Torah Wrestling

Embracing the Marginalized in Jewish
Sacred Scripture and Discovering
Moral Wisdom for Today

Rabbi Roy Furman

For more information and a free discussion guide, visit

TorahWrestling.com

Copyright © 2025 by Roy Furman
All Rights Reserved

The cover art includes a partial reproduction of Rembrandt's drawing, Hagar and Ishmael in the Wilderness.

Scripture quotations are taken from the New Revised Standard Version Updated Edition. Copyright © 2021 National Council of Churches of Christ in the United States of America. Used by permission. All rights reserved worldwide.

Author photos by Linda Horton. LindaHortonPhotography.com

ISBN: 978-1-64180-208-6
Version 1.0

Cover design by Rick Nease
RickNeaseArt.com

Published by
Read the Spirit Books, an imprint of Front Edge Publishing
42807 Ford Road
Canton, MI, 48187

Front Edge Publishing books are available for discount bulk purchases for events, corporate use, and small groups. Special editions, including books with corporate logos, personalized covers, and customized interiors are available. For more information, contact Front Edge Publishing at info@FrontEdgePublishing.com.

Praise for *Torah Wrestling*

In *Torah Wrestling*, Rabbi Roy Furman offers a series of scriptural meditations that are fearless and provocative and thus faithful in the best sense—to the text, the people, and God. Rabbi Furman's willingness to wrestle with Torah and challenge traditional interpretations—and the text itself—reflects the religious leader's obligation to guide his/her people into the highest and best understanding of what it really means to be God's people. I learned a very great deal from this book, which must be read to the very end—the author's personal meditations in the last two selections are especially poignant.

The Rev. Dr. David P. Gushee, Distinguished University Professor of Christian Ethics, Mercer University; Chair of Christian Social Ethics, Vrije Universiteit, Amsterdam; and author of *Introducing Christian Ethics* and *Changing Our Mind*.

Rabbi Roy Furman brings to new life the words of the ancient sage Ben Bag-Bag: "Turn Torah over, and turn it over again, for everything is in it. Reflect on it through all the stages of your life." Whether you have been wrestling with Torah for many years or are coming to Torah for the first time, Rabbi Furman's innovative insights into familiar and not so familiar stories will not only intrigue you, but also empower you to challenge some of the moral issues of our time. And you will continue to come back to these interpretations as you turn Torah over again and again.

Rabbi Laura Geller, Rabbi Emerita of Temple Emanuel of Beverly Hills and co-author of *Getting Good at Getting Older*.

In *Torah Wrestling*, Rabbi Roy Furman enters into an honest, sensitive, and sometimes difficult dialogue with troubling texts from Scripture. For Furman as a committed Jew, the Bible's authors are not simply scribes from distant antiquity. They are members of his own religious community, neighbors whom he visits weekly or daily as he studies and chants their words. Mindful of Leviticus 19:17's command that at times we have a responsibility to reprove our neighbors (just as they have a responsibility to reprove us), Furman lovingly but candidly reproves Torah—always on the basis of other teachings found in that same Torah. Furman also shows how Israel's sacred texts wrestle with themselves and thus invite us to engage them in discussion and argument as well. His approach to Torah-wrestling is a profound continuation of the process of Torah itself.

Ben Sommer, professor of Bible at Jewish Theological Seminary in New York and author of *Jewish Concepts of Scripture*.

Contents

Acknowledgments xi
Useful Hebrew Terms xiv
Preface by Rabbi Allan Kensky xvii
Foreword *(from a Christian perspective)* by Jeffrey Munroe . . . xx
Introduction xxiv

1. Eve's Courageous Bite
   Parashat Bere'shit: Genesis 1-3 1

2. Dredging up the Drowned
   Parashat Noah: Genesis 6:9-8:22 7

3. Patriarchy Run Amok
   Parashat Va-yera': Genesis 19 12

4. But God Sees Hagar
   Parashat Va-yera': Genesis 21 19

5. Seduction of the 'Sacred'
   Parashat Va-yera': Genesis 22 25

6. Esau Gets a Bad Name
   Parashat Toledot: Genesis 25:19-27:46 30

7. The Silencing of Dinah
   Parashat Va-yishlach: Genesis 34 35

8. Behind Pharoah's Back
   Parashat Shemot: Exodus 2 41

9. Lest Innocent Blood Be Shed
   Parashat Bo: Exodus 11-12 47

10. Every Teacher Needs a Teacher
    Parashat Yitro: Exodus 18 53

11. Was That Golden Calf So Bad?
    Parashat Ki Tisa: Exodus 32   60

12. Out With the Troublemakers
    Parashat Shemini: Leviticus 10:1-3   68

13. Our Inherited Moral Dilemmas
    Parashat Shelach-Lecha: Numbers 15:32-36   73

14. So, Who Gets to Be a Prophet?
    Parashat Balak: Numbers 22:2-24:25   80

15. Star-Crossed Lovers
    Parashat Pinchas: Numbers 25:10-18   86

16. No, *We* Are the Chosen Ones
    Parashat Va-etchannan: Deuteronomy 5:1-7:11   92

17. Scapegoating Your Enemy
    Shabbat Zachor: Deuteronomy 25:17-19   98

18. Our Fragile Ship
    Haftarah for Yom Kippur afternoon: Jonah 1 104

19. Unholy Violence
    Erev Yom Kippur 2000 110

20. Will You Forgive Me?
    Yom Kippur morning 118

Afterword *(from a Muslim perspective)* by Saeed Khan 124
About the Author 128

For Frida

Acknowledgments

In many ways, this book wrote itself. I am merely its midwife, facilitating its publication.

Let me explain. Each of its sections is a devar Torah, a "word of Torah," written over the course of weeks and sometimes months intended for a one-time delivery to my religious community, Minyan Lomdim, an egalitarian fellowship group which meets regularly to pray and celebrate Shabbat, Jewish holidays, and lifecycle rituals.

As I prepared and then presented these talks to my fellow Jews on the parashah—or biblical "portion" of a particular day—I had no intention that my teaching Torah, which is my vocation as a rabbi, would reach other religious communities and individuals, and certainly not that they would be published. But people in the Minyan whose integrity I admire and whose knowledge I respect thought otherwise, urging me, again and again, to publish these divrei Torah. In this way I could make them available to others who might also find them inspiring and valuable as they explore with me these texts, many of which they may already know and understand—or think they do. Eventually my resistance gave way to enthusiasm at the prospect of sharing my passion for studying and teaching Torah and, in particular, the desire to explore and "wrestle" with biblical narratives that present me, and I hope others, with a significant moral challenge.

Hence this book.

At its outset, I would like to acknowledge those people, communities, and personal experiences that, intentionally or not, set me on this path.

My writing and thinking as a rabbi and as a Jew have been influenced by my work with havurot (fellowship groups), minyanim, and Jewish congregations in Los Angeles; Portland, Oregon; Chicago; and Evanston, Illinois; by my Hillel work at the University of Southern California and DePaul University; by my graduate work in the history of religions, ancient Judaism, and early Christianity; by my twenty years of teaching comparative religion and Jewish Studies classes at DePaul; by my training and practice as a clinical social worker; and by my numerous stays in Israel: traveling, working, studying, and doing archaeological work over the entire course of my adult life.

I am thus indebted to many good and wise souls, students and teachers, peers and congregants, who have contributed to my learning and have challenged me to grow intellectually, emotionally, and spiritually. Havruta (partner) study with colleagues and friends has been an ongoing source of spiritual and religious nourishment, most particularly with my long-term study partner, my brother-in-law Rabbi Richard Hirsh. And the more than fifty years with my wife, the brilliant, wise, knowledgeable, caring and loving Dr. Frida Kerner Furman has influenced me in life-changing and life-sustaining ways. This book is properly dedicated to her. I also want to acknowledge that, while not consciously doing so, I realize now that I may have been influenced by Rabbi Arthur Waskow's important 1978 volume, *God-Wrestling*, in developing my own title.

The divrei Torah presented here are mostly drawn from presentations to my religious community, Minyan Lomdim. My family and I have been members of this havurah for thirty-eight years and I am enormously appreciative of its ongoing support and encouragement. More recently I have given divrei Torah at Congregation Mah Tovu, also in Chicago, a group of seriously committed traditional Jews who I have known and respected for a long time. I am honored to have been able to share my teaching with them. In addition, I include here a few longer pieces, sermons as opposed to divrei Torah, that explore in some depth a more contemporary religious or moral concern as it might relate to the Jewish High Holy Days, whether on Rosh Hashanah or on Yom Kippur. These pieces reflect a slightly different way in which I "wrestle" with Torah, but one in which I embrace a commitment to social justice and peacemaking, both within American society and that of Israel. I conclude this collection with a very personal type of "wrestling," a struggle with memories of my father and an attempt to come to terms with our relationship.

I very much appreciate the help and guidance I received in making this publication a reality. Rabbi Beth Lieberman provided some initial editorial guidelines and introduced me to Front Edge Publishing. David Crumm at Front Edge proved to be an exceedingly sharp, erudite, and experienced source of editorial comments and suggestions that helped me further refine my work, preparing it for a wider and far more varied readership than I had ever intended or thought possible. Thank you David.

Rabbi Roy Furman, 2025

Useful Hebrew Terms

You already know these terms? Wonderful, then skip this section and read on!

Adonai	Traditional Jewish substitute for the unpronounceable name of God, often translated as "Lord"
Akedah	Binding of Isaac in Genesis
B'tselem Elohim	In the image of God
Devar (pl. divrei) Torah	Torah commentary (Literally "Words of Torah")
Hachmah/Haskalah	Wisdom
Haftarah	Prophetic reading for Shabbat and holy days
Haggadah	Book of readings and blessings for the Passover Seder
Halacha	Jewish law derived from Torah
Ha-makom	The ('sacred') place in Torah

Useful Hebrew Terms

Havurot	Jewish fellowship groups/alternative synagogues
Karait	Biblical punishment by God by being "cut off"
Kodesh	Holy
Korbanot	Biblical ritual sacrifices of animals or grain to God
Maftir	Last few verses of a parashah for Shabbat or holy days
Mashal	Oracle or parable
Midrash(im)	Rabbinic commentary(ies) or interpretive story(ies)
Mikdash(im)	The ancient Temple(s) in Jerusalem
Minyan	Jewish prayer quorum of ten, or a fellowship group
Mishkan	The biblical wilderness Tabernacle
Mishnah	First part of the Talmud; laws derived from the Torah
Mitzvah(ot)	Divine commandment(s)
Mizbeach	The biblical wilderness sacrificial altar
Musar	Jewish ethics
Parashah (parshiyot)	The weekly or holiday Torah reading(s)
Parashat (...)	(Name) of a Torah portion
Pesach	Passover
Rashi	Acronym for Rabbi Shlomo Yitzhaki (Preeminent 11th c. Torah and Talmud commentator)

Rambam	Acronym for Rabbi Moshe ben Maimon (12th c. philosopher, widely known as Maimonides)
Shul	Yiddish for synagogue
Talmud	Multivolume rabbinic interpretation and discussion of Torah intensively studied in Jewish tradition.
Tanakh	Acronym for the three parts of the Jewish Bible: Torah, Prophets, and Writings
Teshuvah	Atonement (literally "turning")
Torah	The first five books—or the hand-written scroll—of the Jewish or Hebrew bible
Zachor	Remember! Name of the Shabbat before Purim

Preface

As the rabbis of old sought to reinterpret Torah so that it might speak to new generations, so the Torah as taught here by Rabbi Roy Furman can speak to a twenty-first century audience who wish to continue the tradition of "wrestling" with Torah to enable it to speak to our times. I believe that the *divrei Torah*, "words of Torah," in this volume constitute a voice that should be heard beyond the confines of the Lomdim *havurah*, Roy's religious fellowship group, and other communities where he has preached. These *divrei Torah*, elegantly written and composed, are replete with understanding and insights that flow from Roy's learning, spiritual sensitivity and high ethical sense, and from a lifetime spent in serious Torah study.

Roy's *divrei Torah* represent true Torah-wrestling in which you will find him questioning the conduct of biblical figures, including God. Roy is troubled by biblical patriarchy, by intolerance expressed for non-Israelites, by harsh biblical punishments meted out to transgressors, by the suffering of innocents. Rather than walk away from Torah because of these serious questions, as a committed Jew, Roy is drawn to wrestle with the text and seek to give these troubling sections new meaning that can address contemporary Jews and other spiritual seekers. At times Roy appeals to the higher ethic that he believes must animate Torah; at times he calls on us to adopt a different stance from the traditional understanding of the biblical text. At all times Roy's search is defined by intellectual rigor and religious honesty. There is no place in Roy's *divrei Torah* for apologetics or conventional answers.

Over the past eleven years, it has been my pleasure to worship regularly with Roy at the Lomdim havurah, a small but energetic community, whose services are marked by creativity, fervor, and a bent for learning and discussion (hence its name *Lomdim*, loosely translated as "learners"). Central to the Shabbat morning experience is the reading from the Torah scroll and the discussion that takes place around it. The reflection on the Torah portion, the *dvar Torah*, "a word of Torah," is offered on a rotating basis by members of the *havurah*, and is generally followed by lively discussion.

The *divrei Torah* offered by my friend and colleague at Shabbat morning services are truly "events," and one can feel the anticipation in the room as Roy takes his seat at the front of the room and readies himself to speak. Roy's *divrei Torah*, when delivered, are ready to be published. They always focus on one theme from the weekly portion. Rather than selecting a section that contemporary listeners can easily relate to, invariably Roy chooses to address those texts that most modern readers would find problematic, texts that raise profound ethical questions and run counter to twenty-first century sensibilities. Roy addresses the text at hand using various tools, including modern biblical scholarship, traditional rabbinic commentary and Midrash, and intertextual readings in which he reads the portion at hand in light of parallels to other biblical sections.

Part of the genius of the architects of rabbinic Judaism was to establish this practice of weekly readings from the Torah scroll, mandating that each week of the year one portion be publicly read and studied. The strategy behind this mandate was clear: to make the Torah a living force in the life of the community. In following the weekly Torah readings, Jews gain the sense of "journeying through the Torah" during the course of a year. Returning to the same readings year after year enables the worshiper to gain insight with each new reading, and to reflect on how one's own understandings change from year to year. When seen in this way, the Torah becomes a mirror for our own lives.

This volume is an outstanding example of the potential of the *dvar Torah* to draw meaning from the Torah for our day. I know that you will be challenged and enriched by these words of Torah. I look forward to hearing many more challenging *divrei Torah* from my friend Rabbi Roy Furman!

Rabbi Allan Kensky is Rabbi Emeritus of Beth Hillel Bnai Emunah Synagogue in Wilmette, Illinois. He has served as rabbi of Beth Israel Congregation in Ann Arbor, Michigan, and as Dean of the Rabbinical School of the Jewish Theological Seminary in New York. He currently serves as a member of the faculty of the Hebrew Seminary in Chicago. He is author of *Midrash Tanhuma Shmot: A Critical Edition of Midrash Tanhuma on Exodus.*

Foreword
(from a Christian perspective)

As I opened Rabbi Roy Furman's *Torah Wrestling*, I wondered: What's a nice Christian boy like me doing in a book like this? After reading three or four of Rabbi Furman's meditations, however, I started wishing I was Jewish. Not only that, I wished I had been a member of one of Rabbi Furman's congregations. He explores the Bible, in particular difficult passages of the Bible, with life-giving, refreshing freedom.

Rabbi Furman turns traditional Jewish interpretative methods upside down. As a Christian minister, I can affirm the same needs to be done with how Christians view the Hebrew scriptures. Too often, Christians take one of two approaches. Either Christians see Jesus in everything or dismiss the entirety of the Old Testament out of hand.

Every reader brings prejudices and assumptions to the Bible. Because of what Christians believe, they are preconditioned to see Jesus everywhere. Viewed through this lens, the near-sacrifice of Isaac recorded in Genesis 22—as difficult and problematic a story as there is in the Bible—is nothing more than a foreshadowing of the sacrifice of Jesus. Or when the Angel of the Lord finds Hagar in the desert in Genesis 16, some Christians see the angel as Jesus in disguise. Never mind that the Bible doesn't say that. These Christian readers want to see Jesus, so they do. This brings to mind the words of Rabbi Abraham Joshua Heschel: Do you only see what you know or do you actually know what you see? Inserting Jesus everywhere prevents the text from speaking for itself on its own terms.

Foreword (from a Christian perspective)

The other approach tries to dismiss the Hebrew Bible. Through this lens, the God of the Old Testament is viewed as different than the God of the New Testament. The Old Testament God is vindictive, angry, and judgmental. In contrast, the New Testament God is loving, kind, and compassionate. This bias is so old there is a name for it, "Marcionism," which the Christian church labeled a heresy centuries ago. Heresy or not, Marcionism persists. I saw an expression of it the other day in a social media post. A friend, who happens to be a Christian minister (and really ought to know better), was ranting because the results of the recent presidential election had not pleased him. He said something about "Worshiping the Old Testament God in a corrupt Old Testament based nation." I know my friend's heart, and I know he didn't mean this the way it sounds, but it's not far from dismissing the Hebrew Bible to dismissing the Hebrew people. This is a grave error.

In contrast to these approaches, Rabbi Furman raises questions that flip common understandings of these texts on their heads. Was it really so bad when Eve bit that apple? What about those innocent people who died during Noah's flood? And what are we to think about the golden calf Aaron fashioned during the Exodus? Furman brings compassion and wisdom to these well-known stories, even as he pushes us to raise uncomfortable questions about them. He also brings light to lesser-known stories, stories often overlooked but which beg for interpretation. Are you familiar with Cozbi and Zimri? Read on in this book and you will be.

Instead of starting with the presupposition that scripture—no matter how puzzling and contradictory—must make perfect sense, Rabbi Furman begins with this presupposition: All human beings have value because they are created in the image of God. Simple as that. All people, regardless of whether they are insiders or outsiders, regardless of any of the myriad ways we define, catalogue, and separate ourselves from each other, bear the image of God.

When the Bible tells a traumatic story of suffering, Rabbi Furman stands with the oppressed, calling into question interpretations that blame the victim. He understands God doesn't need an apologist or defense attorney and can handle our questions.

I am drawn to this. The truth is, as much as traditionalists sugarcoat it, the Bible is full of traumatic stories. After all, there is a murder in the fourth chapter. If you grew up familiar with Bible stories, that familiarity may have desensitized you to how violent and terrifying many Bible stories actually are. Take the story of Noah's Ark. Have you ever noticed that churches love to decorate their rooms for children with fun and colorful representations of Noah's Ark? Noah must have lived in Africa because zebras, giraffes, and elephants all crowd for space in these murals. But read the actual story in Genesis 7. How is this a story fit for children? The amount of death caused by the flood is overwhelming. And that's only one example. The list goes on and on.

I believe telling our painful and difficult stories can be the first step toward healing and hope. In fact, I believe this so deeply I wrote a book about it. But what is clear from Rabbi Furman's *Torah Wrestling* is that telling our stories without a compassionate listener can be counterproductive. Sadly, religious communities over the years have not always listened to the Bible's traumatic stores with compassion. I'm grateful Rabbi Furman does.

Finally, I have to recommend my favorite meditation in the book—the final one. Surprisingly, this is not a mediation on a particular passage. Instead, Rabbi Furman steps away from Torah to tell his own story, the story of his complicated relationship with his father. He offers this for Yom Kippur, the day of atonement. Yet I think of his meditation also as a midrash on the fifth commandment, the command to honor your father and mother. Every one of us, in some way, must accept our parents for who they are (or were) and forgive them for who they are (or were) not. Many an hour is spent in the offices of therapists doing this. But the ultimate move is the move Rabbi Furman makes. Once again, he turns the tables. Instead of dwelling on how our parents weren't all we needed them to be—can we ask our parents to forgive us for not being the sons or daughters they needed us to be? As I read this meditation, I found many echoes of my relationship with my parents. On the surface, my Midwestern Protestant parents and Rabbi Furman's New York City Jewish parents were very different people. Yet in many ways our stories are the same.

I am reminded of the words of my favorite Christian writer, Frederick Buechner, who said, "The story of any one of us is in some measure the story of us all." Rabbi Furman tells his story with unflinching honesty and we are asked to be his compassionate listeners. That's a gift we can give, and as we give that gift, we will be blessed.

Foreword (from a Christian perspective) XXIII

As you'll discover as you turn these pages, *Torah Wrestling* is full of wonderful gifts.

Care to see when these stories will be read in services?

Bible passages throughout Torah Wrestling are read aloud and preached about in many mainline churches that follow the Revised Common Lectionary. If you care to learn more about when these stories will come up in worship, scan the QR code or follow the link to the most widely used guide to that three-year cycle, a service hosted by the Vanderbilt Divinity Library.

lectionary.library.vanderbilt.edu

Jeffrey Munroe is the Editor in Chief of ReformedJournal.com online magazine and the author of *Telling Stories in the Dark: Finding Healing and Hope in Sharing our Sadness, Grief, Trauma, and Pain.*

Introduction

Were you surprised and intrigued by the chapter titles that will guide us through this book? I hope that the unusually worded signposts I have associated with Bible stories you may have already encountered and perhaps know by heart will inspire you to take this spiritually and morally provocative exploration with me.

So let the journey begin!

As a rabbi, a Jew, and a student of Torah, I find myself drawn to those biblical men, women, and even children who we tend to marginalize as we reflect on Torah portions throughout the year. Here I have in mind such figures as Eve, the victims of Noah's flood, Hagar, Ishmael, Esau, Dinah, the Canaanites, and Amalekites. Along with celebrating Israel's exodus from Egypt, I am mindful of the consequences of that process of liberation: devastating plagues visited on Egyptian peasants, not for their own misdeeds, but for those of their autocratic ruler.

This interest might in some way tell you more about me than about the texts themselves, though I strongly suspect that the Torah's very inclusion of these figures and the problematic situations in which they find themselves is a metamessage about justice and righteousness. The fact that generation upon generation of rabbinic and even modern commentators are so intent on seeing these men and women through a negative and judgmental lens, surely responsible for their difficulties, and even deserving blame for their own suffering, is all the more reason for me to respond to them, and others like them, in new and more empathic ways.

Though I was raised in a modern and Western environment, my questioning and exploring difficult Torah texts reflects a challenge from the second century rabbinic sage, Ben Bag Bag, in Pirkei Avot 5:24 (from "Ethics of the Fathers," perhaps the best-known section of the Talmud and the one most readily available to a Jewish audience, since it is found in traditional prayerbooks):

> "Turn [Torah] over, and turn it over [again], for all is therein. Look into it; and become old and gray therein; and do not move away from it, for you have no better portion than it."

What a lovely metaphor for a "hands-on" and lifelong appreciation of a scripture said to be an eternally relevant source of divine revelation and inspiration! So Ben Bag Bag, and others of his and later generations of sages and rabbis invest enormous intellectual and spiritual energy in studying Torah, questioning or interrogating the text, "turning [Torah] over and over [again]," interpreting it word by word, phrase by phrase, and narrative by narrative, that they may discover answers to questions that, they claim, are already embedded in the sacred text, if you know where to look and how to read it. These "answers"—reflecting an enormous range of interests, from the grammatical, linguistic, and definitional, to the theological, philosophical, and mystical—produce wonderfully creative commentaries that have long been studied as a complement to the Torah text.

As Ben Bag Bag's teaching implies, the questions that one brings to the text and the answers that one "unearths" from it change with the different conditions and experiences of one's life—as we become "old and gray"—and in response to the evolving historical, geographical, religious, social, and economic contexts in which the commentators live.

If you are a Christian reading this book, you may soon discover that these are your texts as well, having been explored by a long line of Christian scholars and teachers interpreting both the Hebrew Bible and the New Testament. Indeed for some of you, the work of the Protestant founder of Methodism, John Wesley, may come to mind as he urged readers to keep exploring scripture through the lenses of faith, tradition, experience, and reason.

In my particular exploration of the biblical texts, I will be guiding you through a traditional Jewish invitation to explore, question, and investigate Torah. In this way, I join an ongoing community of rabbinic colleagues, virtually all of whom lived long before me and in far different worlds than my own, "turning Torah over and over again," struggling to wrest from the ancient yet ever adaptable text a wisdom that addresses the challenges of my time and my world. While I occasionally draw on the creativity and insight of such well-known medieval rabbinic commentators as Rashi, Ibn Ezra, and Rambam, also known as Maimonides, who point out issues and problems with the Hebrew text, my response to those issues and the resolution of those problems tend to be far different than theirs.

Unlike a sermon, however, which seeks to make the connection between the biblical world and our own—commenting on and critiquing our personal, social, and religious lives through lessons derived from Torah—a devar Torah, as I use this term, tries to stay within the larger corpus of Torah, allowing the sacred text to speak for itself. Application of that voice to contemporary situations is then the responsibility of those who feel so addressed. And surely that understanding of Torah and its message will change, and certainly has changed, over time.

As a rabbi and as a Jew, I feel a strong calling to respond to those parts of Torah narrative that demand of me a moral critique. In doing so, I attempt to surface what might be called an internal Torah dialogue that scholars such as Michael Fishbane in *Biblical Interpretation in Ancient Israel* and Benjamin Sommer in *Revelation and Authority* call "inner biblical exegesis." In particular, I will be drawing our attention toward texts that many people find troubling and those that might provide a moral counterbalance. Rabbinic Torah commentators have long contended that Torah is not to be understood as a strictly chronological record of events. In that tradition, I, too, explore specific narratives within the context of the entire Torah, referring, as necessary, to sections preceding a particular Torah portion and those that come later.

How does this internal Torah dialogue work? For example, when I read of Eve's eyes being opened to wisdom upon eating the fruit of the Tree of Knowledge of Good and Evil, I see Hagar, whose eyes are similarly opened to life-giving waters; when I read of Dinah and Shechem and the forbidden nature of their relationship, I think of the star-crossed lovers Cozbi and Zimri; with the tale of Lot's daughters and their decision to lie with their father, I recall Tamar's resorting to disguise to lie with Judah, and even Ruth with Boaz; and the deaths of Nadab and Abihu are, for me, a foreshadowing of that which befalls Korach and his band of rebels.

Comparative readings such as these provide the reader and student of Torah with a richer, deeper, and more challenging understanding of the themes and values in Torah, as they are developed and expanded parashah by parashah. Even material in Ketuvim (Writings, the third section of the Hebrew Bible) for example, may echo and perhaps even influence the editor of a text in Bamidbar (the Book of Numbers), as with Ezra's concern with intermarriage among those returning to Jerusalem from Babylon.

I do not, however, embrace the traditional Jewish religious view that privileges Torah as divine in origin and wonderfully encoded with a revelatory underpinning. I see it, rather, as humanly authored and constructed within a particular historical and cultural context. At times, I suggest the influence that a historical event may have had on scripture and its editing, though I try and do so, to the extent possible, from inside the Tanakh—an acronym for the Hebrew Bible made up of Torah, Prophets and Writings.

Nevertheless, Torah for me is kadosh, "holy," in that my mind and spirit distinguish it from all other writings, not as inerrant and divine, but as a uniquely important part of my Jewish and human identity, and that of my religious community. Consequently, my working on the text is, in a way, an exploration, and even a critique, of myself, Jewishly, spiritually, and ethically. Just as one is commanded in Torah to "reprove your kinfolk" for unacceptable moral actions (Leviticus 19:17) there is, for me as well, the command: "reprove your Torah" when it seems to reflect what are unacceptable ethical values. I have thus come to that point in my ongoing study of Torah and the accumulated Jewish and human experiences of my life where both religious and ethical readings of Torah are inseparable and mutually reinforcing necessities.

It is true, I think, that all commentators approach Torah with a measure of subjectivity that reflects the religious and theological perspectives of their historical locations and their individual convictions, though whether they are aware of such influences on their work, or wish to acknowledge them if they are, may be an entirely different matter. I can only acknowledge that my own location and subjective angle of vision is that of a twenty-first century man, Jewishly progressive, and university educated American, influenced by the Enlightenment value of questioning authority and its more recent political and social manifestation of post-1960s America. As a Jew, I live with the ongoing perception that mine is both a post-Holocaust world, and one in which a Jewish state is, finally, a reality. Though that reality, as with all nation-states, may be a flawed and challenging one, I am concerned about and committed to Israel's well-being and vitality and that of her people. My time spent living, studying, and working in Israel has surely had an abiding impact on my life. Beyond this, my participation in non-hierarchical, egalitarian, inclusive, and participatory Jewish communities throughout my entire rabbinic career and most of my adult Jewish life has played a significant role in forming my rabbinic and Jewish identity.

As we undertake this journey together, I will try my best to acknowledge my subjective perceptions and, as much as possible, "bracket out" those religious and cultural biases and perspectives that might get between me and the Torah itself. Indeed, through the process of writing divrei Torah, I am, in a way, attempting both to enter the text as it is, and to react to it, surfacing issues that I think are important and with which I might need to struggle, hence the name of this work, *Torah Wrestling*.

It is also important to note that Torah and the subsequent books of Jewish sacred scripture are, of course, in Hebrew, and it is through that language that we may achieve a greater understanding of the subtle implications of the text than would be the case with only an English translation. Thus, the original presentation of these divrei Torah to my religious communities made frequent use of Hebrew. For this book, however, I have largely presented those verses only in English with occasional use of Hebrew in transliteration to indicate the nuance of the Hebrew original. While there are numerous options for English translations of Torah, I have chosen to use the New Revised Standard Version Updated Edition, building on previous versions that may be familiar to readers, and one of which I used, years ago, in teaching a Jewish Bible course at DePaul University. I am particularly impressed with the scholarship that underlies this translation—the result of a process that, as its introduction says, "involves scores of scholars and leaders from multiple faith communities, inclusive of gender and ethnic identities, with the unwavering goal to render an accurate version of original source texts into the most current understandings of contemporary language and culture."

Through my study of Torah and the process of creating divrei Torah, I find myself, almost in a mystical sense, connected to my religious and scholarly antecedents, both those who created Torah, and those who preserved it through the millennia with their study and their attempt to interpret its truth for themselves and for those whom they teach and influence. I would hope that my teaching of Torah through this writing and sharing of divrei Torah is an honorable complement to their work and lives.

While the commentaries in this book were originally intended for Jews within a Jewish liturgical setting, I am pleased and honored to have this opportunity to address, as well, a broader community from other faith traditions who seek moral guidance and spiritual sustenance from sacred scripture and are prepared to journey with me as we wrestle with an ancient but ever challenging Torah.

Eve's Courageous Bite

Each year, following the fall High Holy Days of Rosh Hashanah (the Jewish New Year), Yom Kippur, and the harvest festival of Sukkot—our Torah scrolls are rolled back from the death of Moses to the creation of the world. We begin once again our annual journey through this sacred text. Our concern in this chapter is with the beginning of Bere'shit, the Book of Genesis. Torah opens with men and women created as equal beings. However, the second chapter undercuts that equality—and the third is a tale of resistance. That chapter deserves our close attention. Our focus is on Genesis 1-3.

Parashat Bere'shit

"Torah speaks to us saying: Interpret me!" Thus the eleventh century rabbi Rashi begins his commentary on our parashah for this Shabbat, Bere'shit. Why, he asks, would the Law Book of Israel (the Torah) begin with Bere'shit ("In the Beginning," or Genesis), the creation of the world, and not with the laws of Passover in the twelfth chapter of Exodus. That's a good question, to be followed by many others.

Torah may be a given, but it is a given that may need to be questioned. Why do the first two chapters of Torah contain two different, even contradictory accounts of creation? Why two versions of the creation of human beings? Why two different, even antithetical, stories of the creation and essential nature of the first woman?

Answers to these questions are wide-ranging. Modern biblical scholars see such differences reflecting various historical sources. Though long ago edited into one Torah, the two accounts retain different stylistic elements, including different names for God: first Elohim (God) in chapter 1, then Adonai Elohim (Lord God, or better, Adonai God) in chapter two. Traditional Jewish commentators see Torah as a unified revelation of God and see such differences as manifestations of God's word. One particular, and rather fanciful, explanation for two versions of the creation of woman is the medieval midrashic tale of Lilith—a woman created in chapter one as Adam's equal and, it is claimed, rebellious, even demonic, mate—necessarily replaced by the compliant and unequal wife of chapter two.

For me, chapter one presents an egalitarian ideal while chapter two is the harsh social reality of an unequal and even patriarchal biblical world. Put in a slightly different way, the creation of the first humans, "in the image of God," shows us the human potential to strive toward equality, while the creation story of chapter two suggests the challenging context within which that potential must struggle to be born. It is this latter perspective that I want to explore in greater detail.

Our parashah seems so constructed as to demand of us, "question me, interrogate me, challenge me." And the model for such questioning of Torah, which, in a sense, is the questioning of God, comes in the third chapter of Genesis with a critical dialogue between the woman and a snake.

But first, let's look at Torah's prologue to that pivotal event. In the midst of the beginning of the creating of the natural world, we get this crucial verse:

> So God created humans in his image,
>
> in the image of God he created them;
>
> male and female he created them.
>
> (Genesis 1:27)

Thus a transcendent God, beyond any personification or visual representation, brings humans, male and female, into existence, creating them btselem Elohim, in the divine image. While there are any number of ways in which we can understand what it means to be created in God's image, Torah itself seems to suggest one with its recurrent phrase: vayar Elohim ki tov. God saw, or better, understood, what is good. And, by implication one would assume, what is not good. So if these first beings are made in the image of this God, they too would see, or understand, the difference between that which is good and that which is not good as a fundamental aspect of their being. That, God then declares, is tov meod—a very good thing.

In chapter two, we get a very different story, one that presents an anthropomorphic and immanent God (now also called Adonai) sculpting a human from the earth, like a potter from clay, a creative and human-like effort:

> Then Adonai God formed man from the dust of the ground and breathed into his nostrils the breath of life, and the man became a living being.
>
> (2:7)

So this Adonai God constructs humans unequally, with the woman an afterthought, a derivative being, birthed from the rib or side of an arguably male creature that he not be lonely:

> So Adonai God caused a deep sleep to fall upon the man, and he slept; then he took one of his ribs and closed up its place with flesh. And the rib that Adonai God had taken from the man he made into a woman and brought her to the man. Then the man said, "This at last is bone of my bones and flesh of my flesh; this one shall be called Woman, for out of Man this one was taken."
>
> (2:21-23)

No longer are they the indigenous creatures of chapter one, created as part of the natural world, beings reflecting God's understanding of that which is good. That knowledge now seems prohibited.

> And Adonai God commanded the man, "You may freely eat of every tree of the garden, but of the tree of the knowledge of good and evil you shall not eat, for in the day that you eat of it you shall die."
>
> (2:16-17)

Death, however, is not the real issue here, at least not on a literal level, for they will come to know soon enough that all beings are mortal. But rather, as the snake will say to the woman, that upon eating the forbidden fruit "your eyes will be opened, and you will be like God, knowing good and evil." (3:5) That is, they would become, as creatures originally created in God's image, able to see, as God does, the difference between that which is good, and that which is bad, without relying on an external authority to parcel out that knowledge.

The events of chapter three and the character of the serpent are, I think, clarifying, as "the serpent was arom, more 'shrewd' than any other wild animal that Adonai God had made." (3:1) But why a serpent in the first place, and what does the label arom imply?

In the mythologies and religions of the ancient world, a serpent often appears as the guardian of sacred spaces, or as a creature entwined about a tree of life within a holy grove. It is seen as a symbol of fertility or a creative life force, but also one of healing, rebirth, transformation, and immortality. These latter characteristics were due, in part, to a snake's unique capacity to shed and regenerate its skin, thus making it a symbol of death and rebirth.

Then, in this account, the woman—as a consequence of her engagement with this serpent—is likewise said to be arom, that is, one who is like the serpent. That is to say she also is "shrewd"—and not the lame and unhelpful "naked" of most translations. Having encountered a symbol of transformation and rebirth, she herself is transformed and, as if reborn, is now named Hava, Eve, "mother of all the living."

I want to make clear that I do not think that a snake has the capacity to speak, whether in Hebrew or any other language, or that a woman can actually understand snake speech, at least not on a literal level. But their encounter provides us with an arresting text. The dialogue between a serpent and a woman prefigures, in a way, the much later argumentation style of the Talmudic tradition, in which one rabbi patach (opens) with a question and another responds with a logical counterpoint, and so on, back and forth, until the issue is resolved, or dropped as the text moves on to another topic. Of course, for many centuries, women were excluded from this tradition and from studying that text, which makes this exchange of views at the very outset of Torah all the more surprising and important.

Clearly, we are not talking about the traditional understanding of a woman, or an ordinary serpent for that matter. If we approach this story on a metaphoric level, we can see it as a woman's profound and daring internal debate—she being both woman and serpent. That, to me, suggests a deeply meditative and consciousness raising experience in which she awakens to that knowledge and wisdom that was potent within her in the first place. And that awareness frees and empowers her to make decisions affecting her own life, the life of her partner, and their common future. To do otherwise, she realizes, is to court a death of the spirit, if not of the body.

First, she questions the nature of the forbidden fruit. From which tree does it come? What exactly is the prohibition? What are the consequences of disobedience? And, finally: Why do I find it so compelling? In fact, its attraction here has little if anything to do with matters of physical appetite and aesthetics, it being "good for food and a delight to the eyes," (3:6)—but precisely because it addresses a deeper need, one that promises an opening of the eyes which we call enlightenment. For it is only when she understands that she can touch that tree if she wants to—and can eat of that "fruit" if she so desires—that she can take her first step on the road to the self-empowerment and the knowledge that would otherwise have been denied her.

Then there is no holding back such an appetite—and she bites in, strongly and with confidence. So much for the compliant woman desired in some aspects of the Jewish tradition! So much for the secondary creation of an unequal being!

This is a woman of agency, choosing to confront the restrictions of her time and place, even risking punishment to do so, for hers is a path, as our text says, l'haskil, that leads to wisdom. Then she shared that "fruit" with the male being who seemed unable or unwilling to take it on his own initiative. If that behavior is said to be "sinful," then she would have to redefine the meaning of the word "sin" and reject the power of others to impose a definition upon her. For eating the fruit proved to be a beneficial and perhaps necessary act, given the narrative in Torah that followed. Thus, upon eating the fruit, "the eyes of both of them tipakachna, were opened." (3:7)

The renowned commentator Rashi supports this with his observation that the Hebrew word tipakachna has nothing to do with physical sight, but rather, as he says, "scripture speaks here with reference to hachmah, intelligence of the mind's eye." (Rashi to verse 3:7)

To this the Rambam (Maimonides) adds that "they received a new faculty whereby they found things wrong which previously they had not regarded as wrong." (Rambam: *Guide for the Perplexed* Part I 2:1)

We have, then, implicit in our Hebrew text and explicit in these commentaries, an affirmation of the first chapter of Genesis, that all humans, having been created in the image of God, do indeed have the capacity to understand the difference between right and wrong. And what is now regarded as "wrong" is that which is conveyed in the "curse" of Eve at the chapter's conclusion: "Your desire shall be for your husband, and he shall rule over you." For that inequality of a man and a women would be the unacceptable consequence of remaining in Eden.

So now these first humans must, not as a "curse" or punishment but of moral necessity, leave the garden of their creation which was paradise in name only, with its constricted definition of what a woman was and what she could or could not say, or do, or even think. But clothed in garments of wisdom and courage they, and those who came after them, would make their uncertain way forward, not knowing that they would—after much time and trial—evolve into a people knowing and doing what is right and good, a people who would carry forward the model of Eve's "courageous bite" to struggle for the radical equality of all those created "in the image of God."

Dredging up the Drowned

Noah's flood is a classic tale of blaming the victim—those who died as a consequence of a global catastrophe. He or she or they suffer, even die—and they deserve to do so. It is a sign of God's displeasure. That biblical thinking is, unfortunately, still with us. I contest it. Sixty-five years ago, this Torah section was my bar mitzvah portion. In the Orthodox synagogue we belonged to, I was not given the opportunity to deliver a devar Torah. Better late than never, I suppose. And this date is exactly the sixtieth yahrzeit (anniversary of the death) of my dear grandmother Sarah, (zihrona l'veraha—may her memory be for a blessing). I dedicate this devar Torah to her memory. For this chapter, we will focus on Genesis 6:9-8:22.

Parashat Noah

"The Drowned and the Saved," as Primo Levi titled one of his Holocaust writings, would have been a better title for our parashah than simply "Noah." Indeed, I would like to speak up for the unnamed "drowned," rather than Noah and his family who are the "saved."

In the ancient world, natural events, particularly those of a destructive nature, are seen as the work of the gods, as collateral damage to the struggles of heavenly beings, as the random exercise of divine power or merely the caprice of playful gods.

Our Torah, on the other hand, sees such events as providential, spelled out most clearly in the catalog of blessings and curses in the books of Leviticus 26 and Deuteronomy 27-8. Those who suffer are being punished for disobedience to God's will; those who do well are being rewarded for their obedience. Thus we have rain or drought, feast or famine, the presence or absence of disease, earthquakes, floods, or plagues. The very granting of life and its taking are all done at the will of God.

The devastating flood in our parashah reflects the assumptions of this world view: Such an event of nature is surely an expression of God's will, through which the disobedient are punished and the righteous rewarded. The world is said to be filled with violence or lawlessness, thus deserving the complete and utter destruction of all humans, myriads of men, women, and children through a universal flood. The justice of such a punishment is assumed; it is certainly not contested. Bad things happen to bad people, God sees to that. So much for the anonymous "drowned."

"The saved," of course, is Noah, a peerlessly righteous man, it is said, whose saving grace is that, ambiguously, he is said to walk with God. Good things happen to good people, at least from the survivor's point of view. This, then, forms a paradigm that persists throughout the Tanakh: God is inevitably seen as right and just in this moral equation, defended as such by Torah narratives, rabbinic commentaries, and divrei Torah down through the ages. This is what theologians call theodicy, the justification of actions and events in defense of a God of justice and mercy.

But let us turn this story over and think of it in reverse chronological order, consequence preceding cause. It would then sound something like this:

There is an extreme weather event.
It must come from God.
Many suffer as a result.
They surely deserve to.
A few are wonderfully saved from that fate, a reward they deserve.

Human experience, however, tells a far different story, then as now. Good people do suffer; and those who are evil all too often thrive. We might ask, then, where, if anywhere, is the justice in this?

I have been studying the Book of Job for decades. It is, in my view, one of the most theologically honest and challenging books of the Tanakh. Job, as we know, suffers grievously: All he owns is destroyed, his ten children die, and his flesh is painfully diseased, this in spite of his being a wholeheartedly righteous man. This is language similar to the description of Noah. However, Job's friends are only able to see him through the lens of traditional theology: Job suffers. Suffering is a punishment from God. God is just and merciful, only bringing suffering on these who deserve it. Therefore, Job must not be the paragon of religious and moral virtue that he claims to be.

But the book of Job, beyond its surface narrative of a man being "tested" by God, leads us in a profoundly different direction, standing the traditional understanding of God and human suffering on its theological head. Job is not deserving of his suffering, and suffering is not a form of divine punishment. As the great twelfth century Jewish philosopher Maimonides would later put it in his *Guide for the Perplexed* III, ha-olam k'minhago nohaig—the world follows a natural course. Our world, once set in motion, by God if you will, does not deviate from its course, either to reward or to punish. Job loses his property and his children due to fire, and wind, and marauding desert tribes. His skin is afflicted with a naturally occurring disease. His suffering is not due to his behavior but to the morally indifferent consequence of natural processes and harmful humans exercising their free will.

For Job and Maimonides, floods happen, as do earthquakes, drought, famine, wildfires, human disease, and even pandemics. People can choose to behave in cruel and destructive ways—or not. Wars are won or lost by human power or poor fortune. And people, like our Israelite forebears, can be exiled from their land by forces more powerful than their own, and, in time, return there if they are permitted to do so. God neither exiles nor redeems the captives. But that is not to say that human beings, as individuals and collectivities, do not have the capacity to prevent or ameliorate destruction and suffering. Compassion and morally courageous behavior are human choices and can be made even in the most difficult of situations.

I remember watching news films of the flooding in 2005 of the Lower 9th Ward in New Orleans as a result of Hurricane Katrina. Those who lived in the poorer sections suffered most, their homes built in low-lying, flood-prone areas, made more vulnerable by inadequately constructed levees. Those with fewer resources were less able to relocate to safer areas, or to reestablish themselves after the floodwaters receded. The actions of people who had the resources to help those in need were at times admirable and generous, and at other times quite callous and shameful. I still see the photographic images of men, women, children, and family pets on the rooftops of otherwise submerged houses crying out desperately for rescue, and line upon line of the newly homeless waiting in vain for bus transport to places of refuge.

So, when we think of Noah's flood, we do well to expand our thinking beyond a biblical narrative that may or may not have occurred in historical time—or in any way like the story of a Noah or an ark. Let us rather think: "Ha-olam k'minhago nohaig"—the world follows a natural course. For example, climate change warms our planet, increasing the frequency and magnitude of storms, submerging coastal areas worldwide, and producing unprecedented events of drought and famine that are threatening the health and lives of millions of the world's most economically vulnerable.

From this contemporary perspective, a medieval rabbinic commentary on the creation of the world and the charge of humans to have dominion or stewardship over all that lives on our planet (Gen. 1:26) seems prescient: "In the Garden of Eden, the Eternal tells Adam and Eve, 'Take care not to spoil or destroy My world, for if you do, there will be no one to repair it after you.'" (Midrash Ecclesiastes Rabbah 7:13)

It is this that we need to keep in mind while the words of our Yom Kippur Mahzor, the prayer book for the Day of Atonement, which we read each year at the High Holy Days, are fresh in our memory:

> Who in the New Year will perish by flood, and who by raging fires; who by earthquake and who by plague … but atonement, prayer, and justice have the power to transform the harshness of our destiny.

These words which we read each year seem to proclaim that choosing to act justly has the capacity to reach out and rescue those who would be among the literally or metaphorically "drowned." But things are not so clear, in our liturgy or in our lives. And we are not, in this country, or around the globe, equally vulnerable to the vicissitudes of the natural and human world. For the fortune that divides those who suffer and those who don't (the "drowned" and the "saved," as it were) does not divide us evenly, fairly, or justly.

In this post-Holocaust world, as Primo Levy surely knew through his own experience, we are, hopefully, well past notions of just deserts, and blaming victims for their suffering, as if intentionally dispensed by a providential God. We best steer clear of easy but distorted identification with those who do suffer, comforting though that may be, as some of us used to proclaim with folksingers Phil Ochs and Joan Baez in the 1960s, "There but for fortune go you or I, even I."

We must avoid the temptation of excuses that allow us to complacently avoid acting compassionately, proactively, and courageously. Indeed, in the real world of many of our lives, empathy for others is all too often in very short supply.

Such is the moral and, indeed, sacred challenge of our parashah: To heed the cry of those who would be among the "drowned."

If we close our ears and hearts to those cries, the drowning may accuse us—as Job accused those who would deny his claim of undeserved suffering—"I cry out, 'Violence!' I am not answered; I call aloud, but there is no justice." (Job 19:7)

Patriarchy Run Amok

With the mention of Sodom and Gomorrah in this Torah portion, we tend to think of fire and brimstone pouring down on a sinful people deserving of God's wrath and destruction. What comes to my mind, however, is that part of the story in which Lot's daughters are endangered by the actions of their own father. Exploring the unequal and unjust way in which some women and children are treated in Torah can provide lessons we still need to learn in today's world. For this purpose, we will focus on Genesis 19 along with later material in the Book of Judges.

Parashat Va-yera'

Our parashah this morning, Va-yera', contains a number of challenging narratives. Most familiar are the two we read on Rosh Hashanah: the akedah, the near sacrifice of Isaac, and the garush, the expulsion of Hagar and Ishmael, with near fatal consequences for Ishmael. In it, as well, is Abraham's presenting of Sarah to King Abimelech as his sister, exposing her to sexual abuse. Thus, two women are endangered at the behest of the powerful man in their lives, and their children brought close to death. I want to focus, however, on the story of Sodom and the Sodomites and, in particular, Lot's two daughters who are vulnerable both as children and as women.

The situation is well known. Abraham's nephew Lot, his wife, and their two daughters are residents in the city of Sodom, whose inhabitants are said to be "wicked sinners." Lot welcomes strangers into his home, angelic messengers disguised as men. In response, the entire Sodomite male population surrounds the house, demanding "intimacy" with the newly arrived visitors, but Lot, anxious to provide the protective hospitality due male guests in that society, offers them his daughters instead. As our text says:

> And they called to Lot, "Where are the men who came to you tonight? Bring them out to us, so that we may know them." Lot went out of the door to the men, shut the door after him, and said, "I beg you, my brothers, do not act so wickedly. Look, I have two daughters who have not known a man; let me bring them out to you, and do to them as you please; only do nothing to these men, for they have come under the shelter of my roof."
>
> (Genesis 19:5-8)

Here the English translation of the Sodomites' demand, v'neidah otam "that we may be intimate with them," is euphemistic, for there is nothing "intimate" in what they are proposing. More accurately they demand "carnal knowledge," which in this context, means sexual assault. To see this as a manifestation of homoeroticism rather than an act of physical and psychological degradation is to seriously miss the point. This is precisely why sex with Lot's daughters is an unacceptable substitute.

But Lot's behavior in offering his virgin daughters to the hostile crowd is, I think, of a piece with the larger parashah and the patriarchal culture it reflects. Just as Sarah can be exposed to physical and psychological abuse as her husband sees fit, so can Lot's daughters. Even though they ultimately remain unharmed due to the intervention of the angelic guests, the horror implicit in Lot's withdrawal of protection from his children remains with us, and, as one might imagine, with the daughters themselves.

If our text in this parashah doesn't condemn Lot's actions, a later and very similarly worded episode in the Book of Judges does, exposing the real danger that confronted women in such a society. In this later narrative, we are told that a Levite, traveling with his concubine, stops for the night in the town of Givah. What follows is one of the more horrific scenes in the Tanach.

Here, as in Sodom, men surround the house where the Levite and his concubine have found lodging, demanding that the Levite be sent out for their sexual pleasure, and here, as well, the master of the house places the value of male hospitality and safety over that of the concubine and even his own daughter. Thus we read:

> While they were enjoying themselves, the men of the city, a perverse lot, surrounded the house and started pounding on the door. They said to the old man, the master of the house, "Bring out the man who came into your house, so that we may have intercourse with him." And the man, the master of the house, went out to them and said to them, "No, my brothers, do not act so wickedly. Since this man is my guest, do not do this vile thing. Here are my virgin daughter and his concubine; let me bring them out now. Ravish them and do whatever you want to them, but against this man do not do such a vile thing." But the men would not listen to him. So the man seized his concubine and put her out to them. They wantonly raped her and abused her all through the night until the morning. And as the dawn began to break, they let her go.
>
> (Judges 19:22-25)

Again, men demand sex with a male stranger. Again, the valuing of hospitality due a male guest. Again, the offer of a virgin daughter. Again, the appeal not to behave wickedly with the man, as if raping the girl would not be a wicked act. So, the gang of men seems, finally, to accept the concubine as a substitute for the Levite. But the prolonged brutality of the assault suggests that, psychologically, it is but a thinly disguised substitute for degrading and dominating the Levite himself, a weapon with which we are all too familiar from times of war.

The exact repetition of Hebrew phrases in both Judges and Genesis suggests that the dreadful and deadly account of the concubine might very well be an intentional commentary on Lot's actions in Sodom, making them all the more reprehensible. For in both stories we see men as enablers of abuse rather than protectors of the women in their lives. While we would want to see courageous bystanders intervene in defense of the concubine, as the angelic messengers did for Lot's daughters, she received no such aid. The conclusion is tragic.

> In the morning her master got up, opened the doors of the house, and when he went out to go on his way, there was the woman, his concubine, lying at the door of the house, with her hands on the threshold. "Get up," he said to her, "we are going." But there was no answer.
>
> (19:27-28)

In Sodom, Lot, his wife, and their two children are warned of the impending destruction of their manifestly evil city and the consequent slaughter of its men, women, and children. Whisked out of town by the angels, they flee for their lives, leaving behind family members who would not take the warning seriously, along with those who were given no warning at all, reminding us of those who were similarly swept away by Noah's flood. The possibility that "sinners" might be given the opportunity to save themselves through acts of confession and atonement is only raised much later, as the Ninevites do in the Book of Jonah.

From here on, however, our narrative moves in a new direction, one in which women take a measure of control over their own lives. Having been warned not to look back toward Sodom in the course of her flight, Lot's wife does just that. Unable, perhaps, to emotionally distance herself from the plight of those left behind, she stops, and looks back toward the city. Was hers an act of empathy with those about to die? A protest against a punishing God who does not, in her eyes, do justice? An intentional act of self-destruction in the face of her husband's willingness to endanger their children? Any or all of these possible responses to trauma makes sense, at least from our very distant perspective. Her body and her message, Torah says, are entombed forever in the pillar which is, we might say, the salt of her evaporated tears.

Lot's daughters take their mother's independent actions one step further. Though previously passive and vulnerable young girls, they now assert themselves as women, the consequence of whose actions will reverberate throughout Israelite and Jewish history. Having escaped the devastation of Sodom and alone in a cave with their father, they imagine themselves the world's sole survivors. In a desperate effort to procreate the next generation, they connive intimacy with their wine-sedated father, each daughter in turn.

> And the firstborn said to the younger, "Our father is old, and there is not a man on earth to come in to us after the manner of all the world. Come, let us make our father drink wine, and we will lie with him, so that we may preserve offspring through our father." So, they made their father drink wine that night, and the firstborn went in and lay with her father; he did not know when she lay down or when she rose ... Thus, both the daughters of Lot became pregnant by their father. The firstborn bore a son and named him Moab; he is the ancestor of the Moabites to this day. The younger also bore a son and named him Ben-ammi; he is the ancestor of the Ammonites to this day.

> (Genesis 19:31-33, 36-38).

It is ironic, I suppose, that the daughters who were sexually endangered by their father, should now subject him to what we might call nonconsensual sex, though, in the context of the story, it is an act without malice nor any desire for sexual pleasure. Here one notes that the Hebrew phrase used for intimacy with their father is not that of the Sodomites or the gang in Givah, v'neidah, to have "carnal knowledge" with its implication of sexual assault, but rather, venishkava, to "lie down with him," implying a more gentle, even caring, act. Their goal is not to degrade their father, but to maintain his family line.

While we may raise questions about the religious or moral acceptability of these admittedly incestuous actions, Torah does not, perhaps foreseeing the historical consequences of the daughters' decisions. They give birth to two male children, one of whom, Moab, is said to be the father of the Moabites, who, in turn, seemingly tainted by their incestuous origin, are claimed to be sexually promiscuous idolators. (Numbers 25:1)

However, that same line, generations later, leads to Ruth, a Moabite woman, who, widowed and childless and taking her fate into her own hands, joins the people of her mother-in-law, Naomi, and marries her kinsman Boaz. Ruth conceives and bears two male children, one of whom is Oved, father of Jessie, father of David. Christian readers of this book will note that this line of succession continues in the genealogy of Jesus included in the Gospel of Matthew.

Wedded to this story is, of course, the account of Tamar. Her first two husbands, sons of Judah and his Canaanite wife, die before she bears children and her father-in-law, contrary to tradition, withholds his youngest son from marriage. She, like Ruth and Lot's daughters, takes her fate into her own hands. In the guise of a harlot, she manipulates a bad situation to her benefit by luring her father-in-law, Judah, into incestuous intimacy, so she can finally have the children she has a right to expect. She conceives and gives birth to two male children, one of whom, Peretz, will lead, seven generations later, to that same Boaz who marries Ruth. They, then, become the great-grandparents of King David and thus, in Jewish tradition, the progenitors of the messiah.

Yet even here there is, for me, a troubling aspect to all of these stories. Women in Torah are, as we have seen, vulnerable to manipulation and abuse, including sexual violence, by men outside of their own families, as well as within. Those who should be their protectors too often leave these women exposed to harm and degradation.

While we might applaud the proactive measures women take on behalf of their own needs and well-being, as is the case with Lot's daughters, Tamar, and Ruth, these efforts only highlight the way in which women are seen as sexual beings, valued for procreation and, by extension perhaps, the care they give to their children. A woman portrayed in the fullness of her humanity is a rarity in Torah narratives and, as well, in many later rabbinic commentaries.

If we are, then, to find in Torah a sacred narrative that speaks to us in our time and place, we would do well to take up the challenges implicit in parashat Va-yera': Pay close attention to the vulnerability of women and children in society and act on their behalf when necessary; acknowledge the anonymity and even invisibility of women in so many Torah narratives and question the ethics suggested by that void; and explore the lives of Torah's women with an empathy and a sense of compassion that allows us to see them as individuals in their own right and not just as extensions of their fathers, brothers, or male children.

Our parashah challenges all of us to question the patriarchy we have inherited, especially the ways some male behaviors continue to be emotionally and physically harmful to women. In our reading, we should not skip over the horrific stories preserved in our tradition. We should rather remember that the story of the nameless concubine in the Book of Judges is only one example of the calls to action we face even in our day.

But God Sees Hagar

Gathered in the synagogue for the beginning of the Jewish New Year and the Ten Days of Atonement, we are confronted with the complex and challenging story of Hagar, Sarah's maidservant and Abraham's concubine or second wife, forced into service as a surrogate mother for her childless mistress. On the one hand, we have a portrait of an outsider, vulnerable to depreciation and abuse. On the other, we have a matriarch and, I will argue, a rarity among Torah's prophets, a woman and a non-Israelite. How then might we understand the story of Hagar as Torah's call to make atonement for our actions during the year now ended? The narrative begins to unfold in Genesis 16 and continues in the holy day Torah portion of Genesis 21.

Parashat Va-yera'

One might think that our Torah reading for the first day of Rosh Hashanah, Genesis 21, was chosen precisely because it reports the birth of Isaac, thus thematically connecting it to a day said to be yom harat olam, the "birthday of the world." But there is, I think, more to the choice of this Torah portion. Much more. Indeed, the shift in names that you will notice, from Sarai to Sarah and Abram to Abraham (and later, as Jacob assumes the name Israel) will suggest that these characters have undergone a personal transformation, though the exact nature of this change may not be so easy to pin down.

An aged Sarah (no longer Sarai), long unable to conceive, finally, miraculously, gives birth. Isaac will now carry on Abraham's (no longer Abram) lineage, and the divine promise of a great and blessed nation becomes a real possibility. There is no longer a need for her servant Hagar, and Sarah is fearful that her son, Abraham's firstborn child, Ishmael, will assert inheritance rights at the expense of her own child. So out they must go.

The back story to our narrative is found in Genesis 16. Sarai, despairing of ever conceiving at the reported age of 90, goes the route of surrogate motherhood.

> So, after Abram had lived ten years in the land of Canaan, Sarai, Abram's wife, took Hagar the Egyptian, her slave, and gave her to her husband Abram as a wife.
>
> (Genesis 16:3)

What we have here is a difference between Sarai's relationship with Hagar, and that of Abram. For Sarai, she is shifchata, her maidservant, while for Abram, she is now to be le-isha, his second wife (a more literal translation than "concubine"). The fact that Hagar, unlike Sarai, quickly conceives, is not surprising. After all, Hagar is young and likely more fertile, but we can well imagine a change in Abram's emotional connection with Hagar, now that she is to be the mother of his firstborn. So, jealousy might be a factor in Sarai treating Hagar harshly, causing her to flee from the family.

> The angel of Adonai found her by a spring of water in the wilderness, the spring on the way to Shur. And he said, "Hagar, slave of Sarai, where have you come from and where are you going?"
>
> She said, "I am running away from my mistress Sarai."
>
> The angel of Adonai said to her, "Return to your mistress, and submit to her."
>
> (16:7-9)

Here we begin to get a sense that Hagar, in many ways, is one of Torah's extraordinary persons. Her sudden encounter with an angel of God, their dialogue, and the command to "return to your mistress," is a clear parallel with Moses' flight into Sinai, the theophany at the burning bush, and the command to go back to Egypt. And it is eerily similar to the prophet Elijah's flight from danger into the wilderness where, at Horeb, the mountain of God, he hears a "still small voice" ordering him to return and confront the dangers and challenges of his sacred vocation. (1 Kings 19)

Like Abram, Hagar is now promised that she will have a child, that his progeny will be innumerable, and "You shall call him Ishmael," says the messenger of God; "for Adonai has paid heed to your suffering." (Genesis 16:11)

> So she named Adonai who spoke to her, "You are El-roi," for she said, "Have I not gone on seeing after my being seen?" Therefore, the well was called Beer-lahai-roi (Well of the living One who sees me;) it lies between Kadesh and Bered.
>
> (16:13-14)

For Hagar, God is El-roi, the "God who sees me," that is, acknowledges her in her full personhood, unlike the restricted and biased way that Sarai sees her and Ishmael. More tellingly, Hagar adds to this name an interpretation: "Have I not gone on seeing after my being seen?" suggesting that she is now one who sees, that is, a ro-ah, a seer or a prophet.

While Sarai may consider Hagar a person of low status and worth, she is, to the angel of God and perhaps to Abram as well, quite the opposite. Indeed, it is only very briefly and indirectly that God speaks to Sarai, despite her status and import as the first Israelite matriarch. That may be Torah's metamessage here: It is the abused and rejected foreign servant, and specifically, one exiled from home, to whom God appears, with comfort and the promise of a good future. Is this perhaps a subtle prophesy that Sarai's descendants will be abused foreign servants in Egypt, but that God will appear to them with comfort and the promise of a good future?

With this preface in mind, we turn to the near tragedy of today's Torah reading. Sarah no longer has a need for Hagar as a surrogate mother or Ishmael as an adopted son, and, feeling threatened by their very presence, she callously demands of Abraham: "Cast out this slave woman with her son, for the son of this slave woman shall not inherit along with my son Isaac." (21:10)

Even though Abraham ultimately accedes to pressure from Sarah in allowing for the expulsion, we get a sense of his affection for Hagar.

> So Abraham rose early in the morning and took bread and a skin of water and gave it to Hagar, putting it on her shoulder, along with the child, and sent her away. And she departed and wandered about in the wilderness of Beer-sheba.
>
> (21:14)

We can almost feel the tenderness of these actions and the poignancy of that moment: He provides bread and water. He places them on her shoulder. He lifts up the child. He sends her away, perhaps never to see her again. After all, Hagar is the mother of his firstborn, but beyond that she is, I suggest, Abraham's spiritual equal and far more of a soulmate than Sarah could ever be.

Hagar now finds herself again in a wilderness, perhaps the same one where she had previously had a divine encounter.

> When the water in the skin was gone, she cast the child under one of the bushes. Then she went and sat down opposite him a good way off, about the distance of a bowshot, for she said, "Do not let me look on the death of the child." And as she sat opposite him, she lifted up her voice and wept.
>
> (21:15-16)

This echoes and perhaps even predicts Abraham's experience on Mt. Moriah in the Torah portion for the second day of Rosh Hashanah. In both cases, one of Abraham's sons is in mortal danger and, in both cases, a saving angel of God comes to the rescue. But Abraham could certainly have prevented his situation by refusing to offer up Isaac as a sacrificial offering, whereas Hagar was subject to forces beyond her control. Indeed, had the situations been reversed, we could well imagine that she would have argued against a command to endanger her son.

> And God heard the voice of the boy, and the angel of God called to Hagar from heaven and said to her, "What

> troubles you, Hagar? Do not be afraid, for God has heard the voice of the boy where he is.
>
> (21:17)

It is a linguistic set up, of course, for surely God would "hear" the cry of a child whose very name is Ishmael, "God will hear." But just as surely, Hagar would have heard a holy messenger, as she had previously.

> Then God opened her eyes, and she saw a well of water. She went and filled the skin with water and gave the boy a drink. God was with the boy, and he grew up; he lived in the wilderness and became an expert with the bow. He lived in the wilderness of Paran, and his mother got a wife for him from the land of Egypt.
>
> (21:19-21)

Though our text says "Then God opened her eyes," we recall that she is a ro-ah, a seer, who, as she said in her previous angelic encounter, "Have I not gone on seeing after my being seen?" Here, as there, what she sees is a well or spring, perhaps the same Beer-lahai-roi, the "Well of the living God who sees me." This near tragic event in her life now becomes one of spiritual transformation. She is no longer a vulnerable and victimized servant, but an emboldened and empowered woman, able to envision a path through and beyond this challenging moment, capable of deciding how and where to live her life, and how to nurture her son into the Ishmaelite patriarch he is now destined to be.

Though some may only see Hagar as one with the dependent identity of wife, servant, or mother, as is often the case with women in Torah—she is clearly far more than that. As we have seen, she interacts with God or God's angels in ways that spiritually connect her to Abraham, Moses, and Elijah the prophet. In this sense, she is an absolutely unique figure among Torah personalities and particularly among women, including those who are revered as our matriarchs. In fact, she seems to be a holy woman, as well as matriarch to those who will later be called Ishmaelites.

Thus, in Islam, it is as the mother of the prophet Isma'il or Ishmael, that Hajar, as Hagar is called in Arabic, is celebrated. And Hajar's search for water in the Sa'y ritual of the annual pilgrimage to Mecca, the Hajj, reenacts the narrative of our Torah portion—said in Islam to have occurred in what is now the Saudi Arabian desert. Here, participants alternately walk and run seven times between two hills some 1,500 feet apart. Ritually they become Hajar, the exiled slave frantically searching for water for her child, then ultimately finding the spring of Zamzam, the well of our Torah text, from which they drink, a sign that Ar-Rahman, the all-merciful one, will provide for their needs.

So, every Rosh Hashanah, I think about Hajar and Isma'il and the Hajj and its ritual reenactment of a desperate refugee's search for sustenance in the wilderness. And every Rosh Hashanah I wish that we had such a ritual, that we might deepen our empathy with those who desperately need the help and support that we might yet be able to provide.

So at Rosh Hashanah I appreciate a Torah portion that presents us with the image of a strong, courageous, and spiritually elevated woman, able to overcome adversity and, ultimately, take control of her own life. She is just the kind of matriarchal figure to guide us into the uncertainties of a New Year.

Seduction of the 'Sacred'

This well-known narrative, the binding and near sacrifice of Isaac by his father, ostensibly at God's command, is traditionally seen as a testimony to Abraham's faith and his trust in God. I couldn't disagree more strongly, and each year, when this portion is read on the second day of Rosh Hashanah, I do pitched battle against this dangerous assumption. It is yet another example of the vulnerability of children in the Bible and in many societies of the past as well as in today's world. It is also one of Torah's subtle ways of teaching us that the common understanding of the text can be a misleading one, even tragically so. The reading, found in Genesis 22, requires close attention to the Hebrew, particularly the use of the word ha-makom, "the place."

Parashat Va-yera'

I am an equal-opportunity sacred space enthusiast. For me, traveling is an opportunity to seek out churches, synagogues, and mosques, the older the better, especially those with complex histories: mosques and synagogues converted to churches, and churches to mosques. I am drawn to shrines dedicated to healing, their walls decorated with discarded crutches. I explore Confucian and Buddhist temples, Mayan pyramids, Hopi underground kivas, and burial sites in Morocco of Jewish saints visited by Muslim women seeking fertility. In this I am not alone, as humans across the globe and throughout history have felt compelled to seek out places they consider sacred, associate them with extraordinary events and myths, mark them with symbolic structures, and perform rituals dedicated to the most holy.

In Israel, I have encountered rocks, caves, and high points infused with mythic connection. "Over here" sacred ancestors are said to have walked, prayed, and been buried. "Over there" is the spot from which Mohammed ascended to heaven, the rock on which Isaac was bound for sacrifice, and the iconic Wall said to have encircled the mikdashim, the Jerusalem Temples, with their holy of holies.

What is this powerful urge to be in these objectively ordinary spaces?

I do not literally believe the mythic histories used to justify their sacred nature. Nor do I think them holy in and of themselves. Yet there is something about a place to which generations of human beings, sometimes with great effort and expense, bring their spiritual longing and existential needs. Perhaps I, too, am searching for a transcendent life experience, not one of devaykut, of merging with the divine, but one of moral transformation. As a Jew, I find a necessary connection between sacred space and holy action. It is this perception that I want to explore in this chapter.

Not surprisingly, Torah presents us with biblical ancestors drawn to holy spaces: God appears to Abraham at sacred oak trees, and he sets up altars on high places. Jacob marks God's presence at hamakom, the sacred place of his dream, by anointing a pillar. Moses encounters God through a burning bush, in the cleft of a rock, and on the sacred height of Sinai. These were, I suspect, known oracular places. Others, perhaps, had heard divine voices issuing from them, and these biblical seekers of sacred space likely expected to hear them as well.

But Torah warns us that sacred spaces, precisely in their compelling nature, can also be dangerous. On Rosh Hodesh Elul, the beginning of the lunar month before Rosh Hashanah, we read:

> "You must demolish completely all the places where the nations whom you are about to dispossess served their gods, on the mountain heights, on the hills, and under every leafy tree. Break down their altars, smash their pillars, burn their sacred poles with fire, and cut down the idols of their gods, and thus blot out their name from their places ... You must not do the same for Adonai your God, because every abhorrent thing that Adonai hates they have done for their gods. They would even burn their sons and their daughters in the fire to their gods."

(Deuteronomy 12:2-3, 31)

This is a disturbing anti-religious tirade, told from a conqueror's perspective, to be sure. But it does bid us beware of the power of holy places to influence moral action, for ill or for good. Beware of the assumption that mountaintops, hills, trees, rocky pillars, caves, and watering spots are intrinsically sacred, of ultimate value. That is the way of idolatry, we are warned.

Yet our parashah has Abraham hear and obey a voice commanding a profoundly immoral act, a three-day pilgrimage to ha-makom, "the place," there to offer up his most precious possession as a sacrifice. At this point, the holiness he attributes to that voice and that place overcome any parental or moral reservations we might have expected of him.

But is this not the essence of what Torah considers idolatry?

Listen, then, to the terse lines of the Akedah, the "binding of Isaac." It is all about ha-makom, the sacred space, or so it seems:

> God tested Abraham ...
>
> "Take your son, your only son Isaac, whom you love, and go to the land of Moriah and offer him there as a burnt offering on one of the mountains that I shall show you." ...
>
> He set out and went to ha-makom in the distance that God had shown him. On the third day Abraham looked up and saw ha-makom from afar. ... They came to ha-makom that God had shown him. Abraham built an altar there and laid the wood in order. He bound his son Isaac and laid him on the altar on top of the wood.
>
> Abraham reached out his hand and took the knife to kill his son. But the angel of Adonai called to him from heaven and said, "Abraham, Abraham! ... Do not lay your hand on the boy or do anything to him, for now I know that you fear God, since you have not withheld your son, your only son, from me." ...
>
> So Abraham called ha-makom "Adonai Yireh" (Adonai will see) as it is said to this day, "On the mount of Adonai there is vision."
>
> (Selected verses from Genesis 22:1-14)

Now, let's look closely at this text. For three days father and son walk on, side by side we can imagine, not daring to look at each other, their eyes only on ha-makom, the arah pulchana as the Aramaic translation calls it—"a place of sacrifice." It is only on the mount, at the altar, Isaac bound, and the butcher knife raised, that Abraham turns, as he must, to face his most precious and now absolutely vulnerable son, that he sees the tselem elohim, the image of God in that face, for "on the mount of Adonai there is vision."

The sacred aspect of the Akedah is not in the testing of Abraham's faith, as so much of Jewish tradition assumes. The sacred aspect lies not in the silence of ready response to a divine command for which generations of rabbis praise him. The sacred is not in Abraham's enthusiastic willingness to go beyond parental, indeed, human, inclinations, as theologians and philosophers have claimed. And Moriah's slaughter-site was certainly not an inherently sacred place.

The only sacred aspect of the Akedah is Abraham's sudden realization, as he stares into the eyes of his son, that what he was about to commit was an unpardonable act of murder, the most profane of human actions. The holy action was not sacrifice, but the unwillingness to sacrifice, no matter what that voice commanded.

In our tradition, only actions have the potential to be holy, not places, even mountaintops, even places that are said to be where God is seen and God's will is commanded. For Abraham had become an angel, a holy messenger, stilling that hand with the slaughter-blade. God indeed spoke, but only from within the deepest place in Abraham's human consciousness, crying out: "Stop! Stop!"

It is this profound act of teshuvah, of "turning" in atonement, that makes this parashah appropriate and even necessary for the beginning of the New Year. For the lesson of the Akedah (and the Book of Jonah on Yom Kippur afternoon, as well) is that everyone is made in the image of God: our people, other people, our children, other people's children.

Holiness is not intrinsic to a place, but in the potential of human beings to do that which is holy. As Israeli scientist and philosopher Yeshayahu Leibowitz writes in *Judaism, Human Values, and the Jewish State*: "Whoever applies the notion of holiness ... to any human, land, institution, building, or object is engaging in idolatry." To which the early twentieth century Torah scholar Rabbi Meir Simhah Cohen of Dwinsk adds in *Meshech Hochmah*, perhaps to our surprise, "All 'holy' things—the land of Israel, Jerusalem, the Temple Mount, the Temple, the Tablets, are not intrinsically holy; they are not sanctified except by the performance of the mitzvot."

It is fitting, then, that progressive Jewish congregations choose to read from Leviticus 19 on Yom Kippur afternoon: kedoshim teh'yu: "Be holy," not in who you are, but in what you have the power to become. A holy people acts toward the stranger, the poor, and the day laborer with dignity; a holy people takes no unfair advantage of those who are vulnerable; a holy people is not indifferent to cruelties done to others; a holy people purges itself of hate and violence; a holy people treats others as they themselves want to be treated: their children as your own, Ninevites as Israelites.

Holiness is found, not in something we uniquely are, but in what we must strive to be—again and again *and again*. Kedoshim teh'yu, do that which is holy, and the ground on which we then stand will indeed be sacred space.

Esau Gets a Bad Name

Here we have one example among many in Torah where the assumed inheritance rights of the firstborn child are undercut by the seemingly arbitrary favoring of a younger or youngest one. Esau, the firstborn of twins, is depreciated from birth and blamed for his inferior status. Later Jewish tradition builds on this, seeing him as evil. A closer look at the family dynamics at play in this portion and elsewhere shifts that blame in quite another direction. We begin, then, with Genesis 25:19-27:46 and continue with the moving events of Genesis 33.

Parashat Toledot

In this Torah portion, there are essentially five characters. The three that we claim as our biblical patriarchs and matriarch, Isaac, Rebekah, and Jacob, are, in their actions, not the ancestral figures we might have chosen. The other two are marginal to the larger Israelite narrative, yet their behavior and character is surprisingly admirable. King Abimelech of Gerar, approached for food in a time of famine, is protective of Rebekah in a way that her own husband is not. He is, as well, generous toward Isaac, despite the fact that he is a powerless stranger who lied about his wife being his sister. And then there is Esau, manipulated and depreciated in this parashah, who proves to be a person of qualities we might admire in an ancestor. It is his victimization and the actions of those who victimize him that concern us here.

Distressed by her pregnancy with rambunctious twins, Rebekah seeks a divine utterance or oracle. The oracular response is well known, though, on examination, it seems more the stuff of wishful thinking than actually predictive.

> And Adonai said to her, "Two nations are in your womb, and two peoples born of you shall be divided; the one shall be stronger than the other; the elder shall serve the younger."
>
> (Genesis 25:23)

Torah, however, does not really hold with a fate declared by an oracle. Indeed, such prophecies can lead to undesirable behavior, as we will see here. In Torah, humans have moral agency and their actions have consequences for which they are, sooner or later, held accountable.

In fact, the oracle proves to be inaccurate, as the older does not come to serve the younger. If anything, we see the reverse when many years later, Jacob will approach Esau fearful and bowing low, as will the rest of his family. The Israelites who descend from Jacob are not necessarily mightier than Esau's Edomite descendants, much as a later Israelite perspective would wish it to be. So, this introduction to a parashah laden with deception is itself deceptive.

Esau's misfortune, of course, is being born into someone else's story. Even in utero his younger brother tries to impose his will on him, grabbing his heel; it portends, perhaps, a much later and darker struggle with a nighttime spirit in which Jacob again seeks to gain a blessing by force and manipulation. He is, tellingly, injured in that process, poetic justice, perhaps, for the pain he inflicted upon his brother. (Genesis 32)

The blaming in our parashah starts early, however. Firstborn Esau, we are told, "came out red, all his body like a hairy mantle," (Genesis 25:25) as if there were some essential, almost genetic, primitiveness about him further suggested by his becoming a hunter, a man of the outdoors. The fact that he is born red-headed or "ruddy," when seen through the lens of early folk traditions, suggests a man prone to a sinister and dangerous nature, even one which will lead Esau, as Rashi's commentary on this text inaccurately predicts, "to spill blood." Such a one, it is made to seem, is surely a "bad seed" deserving of an inferior status.

Jacob, by contrast, is a plain or innocent man "living in tents," though about him one could claim, in English at least, that one who grabs his brother's heel in the womb is, in essence, a "heel." Indeed, the first real interaction between Jacob and Esau is one of callous manipulation. Esau appeals to Jacob for food, for though he is a hunter, his brother, presumably, has control of the kitchen, a situation that Jacob exploits to his benefit, essentially compelling Esau to forfeit his birthright as a firstborn son.

But the text blames the victim, claiming, unfairly I think: "Thus Esau despised his birthright," as if these two children really have anything to say about future inheritance. The fact that Jacob's actions seem to fulfill the oracle's prediction and thus the will of God do not necessarily make them right.

Even if our parashah briefly shifts to a time of famine and the need to migrate to Gerar for survival, it does so with the same theme. As Esau comes to Jacob in his time of hunger, so Isaac comes to King Abimelech, with both father and son manipulating the situation to their advantage. And so it goes; Isaac deceives Abimelech, saying his wife is his sister, and he, in turn, is deceived by his own son and wife, again generated by a desire for food. Jacob deceives his own father; and he, in turn, is deceived by his children, followed once again by famine and the need to migrate, this time to Egypt. Are these actions only matters of coincidence, or the will of a providential God, or even the natural consequences of character flaw?

Is the resort to deception an intrinsically evil act, or is it merely a ruse, understandably employed by the marginal and the powerless?

Our parashah's most notable act of deception is, of course, the disguising of smooth-skinned Jacob as hairy Esau, to which Isaac responds, in confusion: "The voice is Jacob's voice, but the hands are the hands of Esau." To a direct question by his father—"Are you really my son Esau?"—Jacob responds, "I am." (27:22, 24)

Thus we have our patriarch Jacob, manipulated by his mother into manipulating his father, guilty of lying and deception. Our matriarch Rebekah, once endangered by Isaac's deception, is now guilty of engineering the deception of her husband. Our patriarch Isaac, alas, is manipulated by situations seemingly beyond his control: the binding by his religiously zealous father, Abraham, the fear of powerful King Abimelech, the dishonesty of his son Jacob, and his own diminished sight—though one wonders whether he is really taken in by his son's disguise or just passively bends to the will of others.

Though Esau is the innocent victim in this narrative, he is also its most genuine character. Upon hearing that his birthright has been stolen from him—

> He cried out with an exceedingly great and bitter cry and said to his father, "Bless me, me also, father! ... Have you only one blessing, father? Bless me, me also, father!" And Esau lifted up his voice and wept.
>
> (27:34, 38)

Unlike his brother, Esau is open and honest with his feelings. How can we not have empathy for him and his situation? How can we not appreciate that though he "hated Jacob because of the blessing with which his father had blessed him," (41) his respect and caring for his father kept him from immediately exacting revenge? While Jacob flees for his safety to Paddan-aram, there to marry into his mother's family, Esau remains behind, marrying into his father's clan by taking his uncle Ishmael's daughter as a wife. No wonder he is cast as his father's favorite son.

Upon meeting many years later, Jacob erroneously assumes that Esau is still a vengeful youth, trapped in the anger and disappointment of being deceived by his own brother and mother and the theft of his birthright. But it is Jacob who has remained unchanged from those early days, riven by guilt for his duplicitous behavior and now fearing his brother's revenge, while it is Esau who has matured beyond his once vengeful self, and, unlike Jacob, does not take advantage of his now powerful position. "Esau ran to meet him and embraced him and fell on his neck and kissed him, and they wept." (33:4)

Again, the text moves us to appreciate Esau, as the once-wronged brother responds to the presence of his younger sibling in a deeply emotional and physical manner: he runs, he embraces, he falls on his neck, he kisses, he weeps. There is, I suggest, little room to doubt the authenticity of his welcoming Jacob, a perception emphasized in the Torah scroll by the extraordinary placing of a dot over each of the six Hebrew letters of "and he kissed him."

And, what about the tears that Jacob is said to have shed on meeting his brother? Could they have been crocodile tears? Tears of relief that he at least survived the meeting? Having cautiously prepared for the encounter, Jacob can't wait to escape Esau's embrace, deceptively suggesting that they travel separately and join up again at Se'ir, then heading in another direction entirely, toward Sukkot.

But in time Jacob will have cause for real tears and unalleviated grief, as the deceiver is deceived by his own children who present him with the artfully bloodied cloak of his favorite son, Joseph, his earlier masquerade as Esau now come full circle.

The depreciation of Esau in the Tanakh might well reflect a much later animosity toward his descendants, the Edomites, as when God says, "I have loved Jacob, but I have hated Esau" in Malachi 1:2-3, while in Obadiah, God declares to Edom: "For the slaughter and violence done to your brother Jacob, shame shall cover you, and you shall be cut off forever." (Obadiah 1:10)

Such prophetic utterances, and what is subsequently presented in much of rabbinic literature, distort Torah's view of Esau and excuse Jacob for his moral lapses. But a close reading of our text suggests that the evaluation of these twins ought to be just the opposite: that Esau is an earnest son and genuinely loving brother, while Jacob so frequently plays the trickster that his true nature is hard to pin down.

Jacob, of course, is patriarch of the twelve tribes of Israel, and so we claim him as our honored ancestor, but Esau is likewise a patriarchal figure, as spelled out in the lengthy genealogy that immediately follows the death and burial of Isaac, as if to acknowledge that he is, after all, his father's firstborn son and that, in a way, he carries on the family lineage. Rebekah and Jacob (and subsequent Israelite and Jewish tradition) may be intent on declaring Esau an outsider, one of "them" and not "us." Indeed, Edom is later equated with Rome, and the Edomites with Christians. But Torah itself seems to acknowledge that he is still part of the family, making his descendants, that is the Edomites, kin to Israel.

Jacob, having been blessed upon fording the river Yabbok as Yisrael/Israel "One who struggles with God," is, with relatively few exceptions, still called Yaakov/Jacob "One who grabs at the heel," to the very end of his life. Even then, Jacob, ever the trickster, "crosses his hands" to bless Joseph's younger son, Ephraim, with the blessing of the firstborn. Had Jacob not been so eager to flee from a mature relationship with his older brother, he might have learned from him the real possibility of moral and emotional transformation. Indeed, he might have learned how to truly become Israel.

The Silencing of Dinah

Dinah, the only girl among Jacob's thirteen children, is presented in Torah as a silent, passive, and vulnerable young woman, known mainly for having been raped by Shechem, son of a village chieftain. She is seen as the victim of male sexual aggression, yet is held partly responsible for bringing shame to the family. What really took place between Dinah and Shechem might, however, be something far different, as a careful reading of the Hebrew text suggests. Indeed, the truly shameful actions may be those of her brothers, said to be in defense of their sister's honor. And lurking in Torah's shadow, both here and elsewhere, is the issue of Israelite intermarriage with indigenous people. The body of the story is told in Genesis 34.

Parashat Va-yishlach

Dinah is unique in many ways in Torah, starting with the fact that she is the only one of Jacob's children whose descendants do not form one of the tribes of Israel. Her story, commonly referred to as the "rape of Dinah" is a dark narrative that may well presage Israel's descent into Egypt. The context of this story is Jacob's return to the promised land of Canaan:

> Jacob came safely to the city of Shechem, which is in the land of Canaan, on his way from Paddan-aram, and he camped before the city. And from the sons of Hamor, Shechem's father, he bought for one hundred pieces of money the plot of land on which he had pitched his tent. There he erected an altar and called it El-Elohe-Israel/El the God of Israel.

(Genesis 33:18-20)

What we know about these Shechemites is that strangers, such as Jacob and his family, could find a peaceful refuge in their city, could purchase property there, and could freely attend to their own religious practices. They are, it seems, hospitable Canaanites who pose no obvious threat to the children of Jacob, reminding us of King Abimelech who had provided food and a peaceful shelter in a time of famine for Isaac and his family.

Their welcoming behavior notwithstanding, Jacob keeps his distance, settling outside of the city itself with the intent, it seems, of preventing interactions between his people and theirs, thus preserving a sense of separate identity. As Isaac had assumed that Abimelech did not fear God and was of immoral character, Jacob might have assumed the same of Shechem and its people. Indeed, the whole tale of Dinah might have been designed to warn girls and women of the danger inherent in relationships with non-Israelite men so as to preserve Israelite religious, social, and cultural identity. But Dinah, a surprisingly independent young woman, clearly felt differently about any such restrictions, refusing to keep her distance from the Shechemites: "Now Dinah the daughter of Leah, whom she had borne to Jacob, went out to see the daughters of the land." (34:1)

On her own initiative, apparently, and unaccompanied, Dinah enters the city "to see" the local women, "the daughters of the land." She, in turn, is seen by the leader's son Shechem (not to be confused with the name of his city) who, it is said, "saw her, he seized her, and he lay with her by force," that is, most commentators assume, he raped her, an affirmation, it might seem, of the immorality of his people.

But is this what our text really means? A distinct possibility, one imagines, in ancient times as at present. That possibility should not be lightly dismissed. However, the particular verbs describing the encounter between Dinah and Shechem are used elsewhere in Tanakh in ways that do not necessarily signify an act of unwanted sexual violence. (See, for example, Deuteronomy 21:14, 22:24, Judges 19:24; and 2 Samuel 13:12.)

Could this have been a consensual act between these two? Could just being seen alone together have given rise to a false assumption of their conduct, given the norms of that society? Could it be that this, and this alone, is what occurred, as our text says:

> And his soul was drawn to Dinah daughter of Jacob; he loved the young woman and spoke tenderly to her. So Shechem spoke to his father Hamor, saying, "Get me this girl to be my wife."
>
> (Genesis 34:3-4)

These actions do not necessarily seem those of a male exercising power over a vulnerable young woman. Indeed, they are unique in Torah's describing a man's love and caring for a woman, particularly given Torah's reticence to portray the emotions of its characters. Since Shechem, with the backing of a tribe more numerous than that of Jacob and his family, could merely have possessed her as his concubine, his plea to Jacob and his sons for permission to marry her sounds sincere and moving:

> Shechem also said to her father and to her brothers, "Let me find favor with you, and whatever you say to me I will give. Put the marriage present and gift as high as you like, and I will give whatever you ask me; only give me the young woman to be my wife."
>
> (34:11-12)

One wonders, however, how all this might have seemed to Dinah. From her actions, she appears to have had a reasonably positive expectation of the women she set out to visit. Had they in turn introduced her to the man Shechem? Was she the object of his courting and not his coercion? What might have transpired between them when he spoke to her "tenderly"? Did she talk back to him? Did she reciprocate his feelings? Were they, alas, star-crossed lovers? Would the real concern of her father and brothers be her attraction to him and thus their mutual desire to marry? As biblical scholar Tikva Frymer-Kensky suggests in *In the Wake of the Goddesses*, their encounter may have been "illicit" in that context, but not one of rape.

But here, as elsewhere in a narrative in which only the men are reported to be active and verbal, Dinah's response to her situation is nowhere to be found. Nor is she consulted before any actions are taken on her behalf. Thus silence, passivity, and powerlessness are attributed to Dinah, characteristics we see applied to women elsewhere in Torah and beyond in the traditional Jewish expectation of appropriate female behavior. To act otherwise would be to court familial and social disapproval.

And yet we have that very first word of the story, va'tetse, "and she went out," suggesting that there is a Dinah with some agency that the rest of the story tries to cover over or deny. While such independence might be celebrated and supported in a more egalitarian society, a patriarchal culture and one concerned with tribal honor might see such behavior as promiscuous. Is this what lay behind her brothers' question to Jacob: "Should our sister be treated like a prostitute?" (34:31)

But any liaison, however it might be described, between an unmarried Israelite woman and a Canaanite man would, it seems, be so unacceptable in the eyes of her brothers, that it surely must have been one of coercion. So their subsequent revenge against those who, they claim, sullied their sister's honor would, in their eyes at least, seem justified. For were these Shechemites not immoral idolators, and seducers of men and women into their abominable religious practices, as would later be assumed of all Canaanites?

Underlying the issue of Dinah's "defilement" and her family's honor, however, is the broader question of Israelite intermarriage with the sons and daughters of the tribes they encounter. Thus, we have Isaac's caution to Jacob that: "You shall not marry one of the Canaanite women." (28:1) and Deuteronomy's later charge to the Israelites:

> "When Adonai your God brings you into the land that you are about to enter and occupy ... Do not intermarry with them, giving your daughters to their sons or taking their daughters for your sons, for that would turn away your children from following me, to serve other gods ..."
>
> (Deuteronomy 7:1, 3-4)

And beyond that, there is Ezra's much later concern for the preservation of Judean ethnic "purity" in his address to those who returned from Babylonian exile:

> "The land that you are entering to possess is a land unclean with the pollutions of the peoples of the lands, with their abominations. They have filled it from end to end with their uncleanness. Therefore, do not give your daughters to their sons, neither take their daughters for your sons ..."
>
> (Ezra 9:11-12)

So, the Shechemites' urging of Jacob's people to "give your daughters to us, and take our daughters for yourselves," (Genesis 34:9) needs to be seen within the larger context of this prohibition of intermarriage. Jacob's sons, then, could not have seriously considered a marriage between Dinah and Shechem, and their suggestion that such a match could take place if only the Shechemite males agreed to be circumcised was not only duplicitous but sacrilegious in its use of a sacred ritual to lead the Shechemites into a fatal entrapment. As we read:

> On the third day, when they were still in pain, two of the sons of Jacob, Simeon and Levi, Dinah's brothers, took their swords and came against the city unawares and killed all the males. They killed Hamor and his son Shechem with the sword and took Dinah out of Shechem's house and went away. And the other sons of Jacob came upon the slain and plundered the city because their sister had been defiled. They took their flocks and their herds, their donkeys, and whatever was in the city and in the field. All their wealth, all their little ones, and their wives, all that was in the houses, they captured and made their prey.
>
> (34:25-29)

It is hard to think of a more morally reprehensible act in Torah than that perpetrated by Simeon and Levi, especially if Dinah was not, in fact, raped or coerced in any way. While subsequent violence against Midianites and Canaanites is said to be commanded by God, in this story, these two brothers act on their own initiative. Jacob's rebuke that their actions damaged his own reputation and made their family vulnerable to revenge by other Canaanites seems mild, if not morally obtuse. Of the opportunistic plundering of Shechem and the taking of women and children captive by his other sons, Jacob is mute.

But Torah might be providing commentary on our parashah when it confronts us with a startlingly similar situation. As Israelites are much later preparing to leave the wilderness after forty years and enter Canaan, we are presented with another pair of star-crossed lovers: Cozbi, a Midianite woman, and Zimri, an Israelite who is, ironically, of the tribe of Simeon. They appear before Moses and the people and, on his own initiative, the zealous priest Pinchas, of the tribe of Levi, stabs them to death. (Numbers 25) Later, ostensibly at God's command, this same descendant of Levi presides over the massacre of Midianites, the plunder of their land, and the taking of their unmarried women and female children as captives. (Numbers 31)

I must ask: Are these two narratives speaking to one another? Is the death of this son of the tribe of Simeon and the zealotry of a priest of the tribe of Levi who kills him a commentary on the murderous behavior of their antecedents Simeon and Levi in our Torah portion? Are these later events a not-so-subtle critique of Jacob who did not clearly and forcefully condemn the actions of his sons and so might, in some way, be responsible for actions of another time and place? Is this Torah's challenge to us to confront and condemn immoral behavior, especially among one's own people, lest there be consequences for which we, in some way, might be responsible?

This Torah portion serves as a bridge between the Assyria that Jacob left and Israel's descent into Egypt in the parshiyot coming up in our yearly cycle of readings. So one wonders whether Israel's oppression in Egypt is, in some way, meant to be a corrective that the children of Jacob might experience the suffering they brought upon others and that their descendants might become an empathic people, covenanted to care for the marginalized and mistreated: those who are widows, orphans, and strangers.

Each of the twelve sons of Jacob is, at birth, given a name related to his mother's good fortune in having another son, as population growth was surely crucial to the birthing of a new people. But with the giving of the name Dinah, Torah teaches that the essence of that name—good "judgment" or acts of "justice"—is crucial to the moral growth of that same people.

Behind Pharoah's Back

The second book of Torah, Exodus, opens with a threat of genocide hanging over the Hebrew population. There is, likewise, an incipient women's resistance movement committed to protecting children whose lives are threatened. And out of Pharaoh's own family emerges his courageously righteous daughter, prepared to oppose his murderous decrees, even at the risk of her own safety. Later Jewish tradition would call such a woman a "righteous Gentile." This devar Torah is in memory of my mother-in-law, Sara Karlinsky Kerner, born in Harbin, China. Today is the ninety-ninth anniversary of her birth on December 25, 1922. She was the daughter of parents fleeing Ukrainian pogroms. Our story of rescue and survival is largely told in one tersely worded chapter, Exodus 2.

Parashat Shemot

The declining fortune of the Hebrews in biblical Egypt seems like a dark omen of later Jewish experience. Given protection and a measure of public influence by Pharaoh at the end of Genesis, they are—in parashat Shemot at the beginning of Exodus—seen as a threat by the new regime. There are too many of them, this pharaoh says, and their loyalty cannot be counted on in time of war. The "shrewd" way he chooses to deal with the situation is, we would say, by means of genocide. His initial effort is somewhat secretive, as he enlists midwives in a murderous scheme to kill newborn Hebrew boys. Their actions in response are courageously subversive. Frustrated, Pharaoh goes public, commanding of ordinary Egyptians that they kill the newborn children, as we read:

> Then Pharaoh commanded all his people, "Every son that is born to the Hebrews you shall throw into the Nile, but you shall let every daughter live."
>
> (Exodus 1:22)

One can hardly imagine the terror that such an order would generate within Hebrew families and the challenge it would present to any who would dare resist as did the midwives. Yet there are some, a very few perhaps, willing to risk disobeying a royal degree, as narrated in the first ten tightly constructed verses in the second chapter of Exodus. While the women who take this risk might seem marginal to the larger Israelite story, they are, I suggest, crucial to its moral development.

> Now a man from the house of Levi went and married a Levite woman. The woman conceived and bore a son, and when she saw that he was a fine baby, she hid him three months. When she could hide him no longer she got a papyrus basket for him and plastered it with bitumen and pitch; she put the child in it and placed it among the reeds on the bank of the river.
>
> (2:1-3)

It is the Levite woman who is the main actor here. She sees how precious the child is, she hides him, she prepares the basket, she closes him within it, and she places it among the reeds. The verses that follow reflect these same actions in reverse, as Pharaoh's daughter sees the basket, removes it from the reeds, opens it, and sees the child within. The verbal balance here seems almost like a practiced "handoff," one woman to another, one mother to another, the placing of the child in the reeds a calculated artifice. Indeed, the language of the text suggests that the basket was placed in the precise spot where the princess would likely find it, with the child's sister making sure that the connection was expeditiously made. The birthing symbolism of a womb-like basket and a child pulled forth from the life-giving waters of the Nile seems clear: He is given a new lease on life, a second birth.

> The daughter of Pharaoh came down to bathe at the river, while her attendants walked beside the river. She saw the basket among the reeds and sent her maid to bring it. When she opened it, she saw the child. He was crying, and she took pity on him. "This must be one of the Hebrews' children," she said.
>
> (2:5-6)

Pharaoh's daughter is said to "take pity" on a crying child, one whose very existence now lay solely in her hands. She is moved to comfort and rescue him, but her actions almost seem premeditated. How is it that she happens to go down to the Nile at precisely that time and at that spot? Why were her maidens sent on a scouting expedition along the riverbank—as if searching for something they knew to be hidden among the reeds?

Was it pure chance that they find a basket, an abandoned child within, or was it not expected that desperate Hebrew mothers would place their infant boys in the Nile with the hope that they might happen upon a more secure future than they themselves could provide? Clearly the princess and her maid servants would have known of Pharaoh's very public and murderous command and were prepared to act in defense of mortally endangered babies, knowing the risks they might be taking in doing so.

But what, we ask, might have motivated one raised within an authoritarian court and society to disobey a royal command and save the life of a Hebrew infant?

Was this a commitment on her part to do justice within a profoundly unjust context? Could she have been exposed to teachings within the Egyptian world, religious or otherwise, that commanded protection of those marginalized within her society, of whom the Hebrews would be a primary exemplar? Was she possibly raised by a mother who modeled altruistic behavior, a moral counterbalance to her father's immoral propensities? The answers to these questions remain buried beneath the spare language of our few verses, though Jewish tradition is all too quick to assume that she had converted to Judaism and thus felt compassion toward a Jewish child, an assumption made of the midwives as well.

> Then his sister said to Pharaoh's daughter, "Shall I go and get you a nurse from the Hebrew women to nurse the child for you?"
>
> Pharaoh's daughter said to her, "Yes."
>
> So the girl went and called the child's mother.
>
> Pharaoh's daughter said to her, "Take this child and nurse it for me, and I will give you your wages."
>
> So the woman took the child and nursed it.
>
> (2:7-9)

The apparent spontaneity of the rescue plan and the ease with which it is executed suggests that something else was going on, something more carefully thought out in advance, in cooperation, perhaps, with the baby's sister and birth mother, so that the child's nursing would be minimally disrupted. Indeed, the collaboration of numerous women in this narrative, including the midwives in the previous chapter, suggests that a more widespread effort of resistance might have been afoot.

> When the child grew up, she brought him to Pharaoh's daughter, and he became her son. She named him Moses, she said, "because I drew him out of the water."
>
> (2:10)

Upon being weaned, the child is formally adopted by Pharaoh's daughter, who gives her son a common Egyptian name Mose meaning "son of," though it is Hebraicized in our text to Moshe, "drawing out." As Torah simply says of the years he was being nursed, "the child grew up," so does the very next verse say that "some time after that when Moses had grown up," this time after a period of some forty years according to the way Torah seems to divide up his life. What influences might have shaped the child and the man he grew to be, educated as a prince in the royal court, and exposed to the values that had informed his adoptive mother's life, along with the model of her moral behavior? About this our text is opaque. However, we soon see his moral outrage surfacing in the face of injustice.

> One day after Moses had grown up, he went out to his people and saw their forced labor. He saw an Egyptian beating a Hebrew, one of his own people. He looked this way and that, and seeing no one, he killed the Egyptian and hid him in the sand.
>
> (2:11-12)

We can only guess how Moses knew he was kin to a Hebrew slave. Was the woman who saved his life also committed to preserving his religious identity? Was it solely a sense of a shared lineage that drew him to the slave's defense? Or was he simply outraged at the injustice of an overseer's brutality and would as well have come to the rescue of a non-Hebrew, as he indeed does but a few verses later in rescuing Jethro's defenseless daughters from the bullying of nearby shepherds? For was this not the lesson of his adoptive mother's actions in defense of the helpless baby he had been? But if this was the lesson that he learned from Pharaoh's daughter, he did not learn it fully enough, else he surely would have opposed the plague in which "every firstborn in the land of Egypt shall die."

I do not know if the actions attributed to Pharaoh's daughter reflect a historical truth, but they certainly reflect a moral and a universal one: People have the capacity to act in defense of those who are endangered, in spite of those forces and influences and even rationalizations that would have them do otherwise.

So let me conclude by telling a story: It is the story of a woman, a Jewish woman, who gave birth to a beautiful boy in a time and place where Jewish babies were being rounded up and murdered. Desperate to save her son's life, she approached a non-Jewish neighbor, begging her to take the boy and adopt him as her own, which she did. The boy was given a non-Jewish name and raised as a non-Jew. But the boy was also taught that he had another mother and another religion. When the danger had passed, the boy returned to his mother and his people.

If I were hearing this story for the first time, I could not tell you whether that birth mother was a Levite in ancient Egypt, or a Jew in Nazi-occupied Europe. Neither could I tell you whether the adoptive mother was the daughter of a pharaoh or a Christian Polish woman.

Maybe that distinction doesn't matter. Maybe it is the same story after all.

Alas, the story Jewish history tells does not always have such a good ending. For rescuers of our people, and others so endangered, have long been too few and those in need of rescue far too many.

Yet each year, with the reading of parashat Shemot, a tsadeket, a righteous Egyptian woman, challenges us anew with her story.

Lest Innocent Blood Be Shed

The dramatic tale of Israel's liberation from Egyptian bondage and the ten plagues that are said to make that possible has a dark underbelly, the plague of the killing of the firstborn Egyptians whose only "sin" would be their living under a tyrannical pharaoh's "hard-hearted" rule. If the Israelite slaves suffered through hard labor and beatings, Egyptian men, women, and children might have done so as well. Now they face undeserved slaughter. But the story, and particularly its joyous celebration at the Passover Seder, raises disturbing questions, as it should. And I build on this concern at the very end of this devar Torah. Our main focus, then, will be on Exodus 11-12, a particularly important part of Exodus, as it initiates the Jewish calendar and the commandments related to the observance of Passover.

Parashat Bo

I wrote this devar Torah during the second consecutive COVID pandemic year in which the account of plagues in biblical Egypt resonated in powerful ways in our community. In parashat Bo, we encounter the final plague brought by God on the Egyptians, the tipping point for Israel's liberation and, as well, the suffering of those whose misfortune it is to be ruled by a hard-hearted pharaoh. To this day, we read of the killing of firstborn Egyptians—and, as we do, we need to wrestle from this text a sacred teaching and a moral challenge.

Pharaoh is the prototype of a cruel dictator who not only resists Israel's liberation efforts but is seemingly indifferent to the suffering of his own people. For it is mostly the ordinary men, women, and children of Egypt upon whom the plagues are visited.

We know this list of disasters so well that their names trip effortlessly from our tongues around the Passover Seder table—blood, frogs, lice, wild beasts, pestilence. We rarely pause to consider the implications for people subjected to them: The life-giving waters of the Nile no longer support life; frogs pile up in heaps and stink; vermin come upon humans and beasts alike; cattle die; hail destroys the grasses and trees; locust swarms darken the land consuming all remaining crops; and then comes the Plague of All Plagues, an epidemic mortally sickening all firstborn.

While every Egyptian family was struck in some way and the wailing of survivors is said to have been unimaginable, the Torah does not detail the other deaths likely resulting from the first nine plagues, but surely there would have been many. For the consequences of this succession of disasters are all too familiar to us in today's world: famine, disease, social chaos, and widespread suffering, particularly among those least resilient—young children, the aged, the poor, the marginalized, the disempowered.

Israelite empathy for these unfortunates seems seriously limited, whether out of ignorance, indifference, a narrowly focused nationalism, or joyous relief at the prospect of liberation from bondage, accompanied by revenge feelings against "those Egyptians" who oppressed them. At long last, the hard wall of Pharaoh's heart has been breached! Now, surely, he would "let my people go."

I am asking in this chapter: Where is our compassion for the suffering of these common Egyptians? Consider the injustice! Aim a plague at Pharaoh and you hit his people, what we moderns have tended, in times of war, to excuse as "collateral damage." Even the death of Pharaoh's firstborn strikes at a child who is, at best, only guilty by association. The despot himself is, curiously, allowed to live on. Surely there must be, in a tradition such as ours that commands justice for the stranger, love for one's neighbor, and the proscription against holding children responsible for the misdeeds of their parents, room for concern for such suffering.

The Moses whom we might have counted on to pick up Abraham's challenge to God at the prospect of the destruction of Sodom and Gomorrah: "Will you indeed sweep away the righteous with the wicked?" (Genesis 18:23) is absent here, as is the Moses to whom tradition attributes the characteristics of justice and mercy. Ten righteous souls may or may not have been in Sodom, but surely at least as many were in Egypt, paramount among them Pharaoh's daughter,

Moses' adoptive mother. Was she Pharaoh's firstborn? What about the courageous midwives Shifra and Puah who saved countless Hebrew lives? What of their firstborn, and those of the generous Egyptians who gifted resources to their departing Hebrew neighbors?

This aside, there surely would have been a traumatic memory of Pharaoh's command to kill newborn Hebrew boys. That cruel order would have destroyed Moses' own life had not Pharaoh's daughter seen him as an endangered infant and not just one of "those Hebrews" who are best eliminated from society. Could we not expect Moses—who would have had the altruistic model of his adoptive mother—to intervene when the lives of Egyptian babies were similarly endangered? The first century sage and rabbi Hillel the Elder could, we might think, have had this in mind in declaring, "Do not do to others what was hateful when it was done to you."

Many Passover Haggadahs quote a lovely midrash on the drowning of Pharaoh's charioteers at the Red Sea:

> The ministering angels wanted to sing their song ... but the Holy One, Blessed be He, said: "The ... work of My hands, the Egyptians, are drowning at sea, and you wish to sing songs?"

(Tractate Megillah 10b)

But less quoted is the Talmudic comment which immediately follows:

> Rabbi Elazar [ben Azariah, a first century sage] said, This is how the matter is to be understood: Indeed, God does not rejoice [over the downfall of the wicked,] but causes others to rejoice.

(10b)

It is, we might say, a sensitive God who does not rejoice at the death of fighting men, even those intent on doing harm to men, women, and children fleeing for their lives. But are less sensitive humans permitted, even urged, to do so?

To this day, we must wrestle with this moral challenge: What is the appropriate response to the tenth plague and its slaughter of those who might reasonably be considered innocent of wickedness? Would a sensitive God not be aware that non-combatant Egyptian firstborn are also created in God's image? Would a just and compassionate God endorse the deaths of those not responsible for the deeds and hard-heartedness of a ruler they probably would not have wanted in the first place? Where is the empathy for those parents suffering the deaths of children who could not possibly have participated in the enslavement of Israelites?

Our Torah gives us a sense of just how deep this injustice goes, as we read God's prediction that:

> Every firstborn in the land of Egypt shall die, from the firstborn of Pharaoh who sits on his throne to the firstborn of the female slave who is behind the handmill... [and] the firstborn of the prisoner who was in the dungeon.
>
> (Exodus 11:5; 12:29)

Consider another possibility: Why would our text have the chutzpah to call for the death of such vulnerable and powerless Egyptians as these unless it was for the purpose of stirring up compassion and empathy in those Israelites who should have been quick to identify with their dreadful circumstances?

It is here that we need to pay attention to a peculiar shift in Torah. The tenth and last plague, the killing of firstborn Egyptians, is foretold at the end of Exodus 11, with the expectation that it will come to pass in the very next chapter. But Exodus 12 unexpectedly shifts to something quite different, the Passover ritual: the lamb, the sacrifice, the blood, the shared meal. As important as this material may be from a traditional Jewish perspective, however, it interrupts the narrative flow; indeed, it seems like an unnecessary intrusion in the plague events. It is only after the detailed instructions for Passover are carefully spelled out that Torah returns to the matter of the last plague. A scholarly assumption is that the description of Passover at this point is a later editorial insertion designed to connect a preexisting pastoral ritual to the exodus from Egypt.

Scholars may be right from a historical perspective, but I believe this is far from what Torah is trying to tell us about the meaning and moral intent of this particular sacrificial ritual and the reason it immediately precedes the plague of the killing of firstborn Egyptians.

> Then Moses called all the elders of Israel and said to them, "Go, select lambs for your families, and slaughter the Passover lamb. Take a bunch of hyssop, dip it in the blood that is in the basin, and touch the lintel and the two doorposts with the blood in the basin. None of you shall go outside the door of your house until morning. For Adonai will pass through to strike down the Egyptians; when he sees the blood on the lintel and on the two doorposts, Adonai will pass over that door and will not allow the destroyer to enter your houses to strike you down.
>
> (12:21-23)

Blood is, of course, a powerful symbol in many cultures, signifying, among other things, both life and death. Here, apparently, it signifies the death of sacrificial lambs with the blood-stained lintel and doorposts providing protection from "the Destroyer." But Torah also, and perhaps most crucially, sees blood as a manifestation of life, saying: "For the life of every creature—its blood is its life." (Leviticus 17:14) and "Whoever sheds the blood of a human, by a human shall that person's blood be shed, for in his own image God made humans." (Genesis 9:6)

What are we to make, then, of the phrasing of our text: Adonai, when going through to smite the Egyptians, "sees the blood on the lintel and on the two doorposts"? First God sees the lamb's blood, then spills the blood of firstborn humans. Even as they are marking their doors, the Israelites know a bloodbath is coming. It is, I suggest, at this dramatic point in the plague narrative, that the Israelites are confronted with a most difficult question. Will they think only of their own liberation from Egypt no matter what the consequences for Egyptian children? Or, will they have the moral courage to challenge the God who is about to spill innocent blood, as did Abraham with the impending slaughter of the Sodomites?

> "Far be it from you to do such a thing, to slay the righteous with the wicked, so that the righteous fare as the wicked! Far be that from you! Shall not the Judge of all the earth do what is just?"
>
> (Genesis 18:25)

But the Israelites do not pursue this courageous path. God is not deterred from carrying out the last, murderous plague—and future generations remember and celebrate this mythic moment in Jewish history, as Torah commands:

> "You shall observe this as a perpetual ordinance for you and your children. When you come to the land that Adonai will give you, as he has promised, you shall keep this observance. And when your children ask you, 'What does this observance mean to you?' you shall say, 'It is the Passover sacrifice to Adonai, for he passed over the houses of the Israelites in Egypt when he struck down the Egyptians but spared our houses.'"
>
> (Exodus 12:24-27)

And this, I suggest, is Torah's difficult but ongoing challenge to those sitting around the seder table. Each year, we are called to pay attention to the child's seemingly simplistic but actually profound query: "What does this observance mean *to you*?"

In response, we must confront the upsetting yet essential question: Why did God shed the blood of innocent Egyptians? Why did the Israelites look upon the animal blood on the doorposts of their houses and not argue God out of shedding the blood of humans? Far more importantly, however, is the question: What might we do in a similar situation?

Every Teacher Needs a Teacher

Jethro's claim to fame may be as Moses' father-in-law. But it is as a Midianite priest, a mentor to Moses, and a desert guide that define the absolutely necessary role he plays in the Israelite biblical narrative. Without him, the Israelite wilderness experience might have been a disaster, and their developing religious practice and values might have been quite different. Let's see if the text itself supports such a bold claim. To cover the range of this material, we start with Exodus 18, move back to Exodus 3-4, then onward to Numbers 10. By the way, don't be fooled by the places where Jethro is also called Hobab and Reuel. Torah seems to use them interchangeably and I suggest we do as well.

Parashat Yitro

Here is how Torah describes Yitro's, that is Jethro's, encounter with Moses just prior to the revelation of the Ten Commandments at Sinai:

> Jethro, the priest of Midian, Moses' father-in-law, heard of all that God had done for Moses and for his people Israel, how Adonai had brought Israel out of Egypt. ...
>
> Jethro, Moses' father-in-law, along with Moses' sons and wife, came into the wilderness where Moses was encamped at the mountain of God. He sent word to Moses, "I, your father-in-law Jethro, am coming to you, with your wife and her two sons."

> So Moses went out to meet his father-in-law; he bowed down and kissed him; each asked after the other's welfare, and they went into the tent.
>
> (Exodus 18:1, 5-7)

While Moses is the central figure in Israel's liberation from Egypt and its forty years of wandering—Jethro is his guide and facilitator. The fact that he is an outsider to the Israelite tradition, a Midianite, and a priest at that, might seem odd at first, but that is a necessary part of the story. As a Midianite, he is part of a nomadic people, whose encampments are spread across the same wilderness that the liberated Israelites must traverse: Sinai, Canaan, and Moab. As such, the Midianites knew the ways of desert life, the best routes to travel, and the location of oases that would support the life of shepherds as well as their herds and flocks. They would have religious traditions that make sense in the harsh and challenging world in which they live, along with the conviction that there were sacred sites where their gods could be encountered, mostly high places and mountains. There were, we can imagine, beliefs and practices they had in common with other peoples of that time and place. They would, as well, have a set of values and laws, particularly those that would promote tribal and intertribal cooperation—as Bedouin tribes in that area have long had. And Jethro, as a priest, would be both a religious and tribal leader, one to whom his people would turn for advice, especially in difficult times.

In Torah, Jethro is repeatedly referred to as Moses' father-in-law—twelve times in the first chapter of this parashah alone. As his son-in-law, Moses may well have come to see Jethro as a parental figure, one who could give him the advice that a father would. But the repeated references to a relationship by marriage and the reemergence, as if on cue, of a wife and children from whom he has apparently been separated, suggest that Moses' marriage is one whose purpose it is to promote an alliance between the tribe of Moses and that of Jethro, a widely known function of intertribal marriages.

Indeed, this relationship is symbolically acknowledged as Moses welcomes his father-in-law, going out to meet him, bowing low, and kissing him. Their going into the tent sets the stage for a formal encounter during which Jethro, as a priest, could offer sage counsel to a troubled Moses. In a way, it is a continuation of their previous meeting, which forms the backstory to our parashah, suggesting that there is an ongoing connection between these two and their peoples. Indeed, it seems significant that this meeting is immediately followed by the revelation at Sinai, as Moses' previous stay with Jethro preceded the revelation at the burning bush.

Moses, as we know, flees from Pharaoh's wrath to the territory of the Midianites and sits down by a well. In short order: Moses protects the daughters of the Midianite priest Reuel, also known as Jethro, from hostile shepherds; then, he is invited into the Midianite camp, marries the priest's daughter Zipporah, has two children, and works as a shepherd for forty years. All of which leads up to Moses' theophany and the turning point in the Israelite narrative:

> Moses was keeping the flock of his father-in-law Jethro, the priest of Midian; he led his flock beyond the wilderness and came to Mount Horeb, the mountain of God. There the angel of Adonai appeared to him in a flame of fire out of a bush; he looked, and the bush was blazing, yet it was not consumed. Then Moses said, "I must turn aside and look at this great sight and see why the bush is not burned up."
>
> When Adonai saw that he had turned aside to see, God called to him out of the bush, "Moses, Moses!"
>
> And he said, "Here I am."
>
> Then he said, "Come no closer! Remove the sandals from your feet, for the place on which you are standing is holy ground." He said further, "I am the God of your father, the God of Abraham, the God of Isaac, and the God of Jacob."
>
> And Moses hid his face, for he was afraid to look at God.
>
> (Exodus 3:1-6)

Moses is transformed, overnight it would seem, from an Egyptian palace-dwelling prince to a nomadic shepherd. Over time, he would learn how to survive in the desert, know the location of wells and holy places, and feel a bond with his father-in-law and perhaps with the Midianites as well.

How much of Moses' encounter with a messenger of Adonai, by a bush on fire, and on a holy mountain is a consequence of being immersed in Midianite culture and being the son-in-law of their priest, can only be a matter of conjecture. But the sharing of physical space for what seems to be a very considerable amount of time would, we might well expect, result in a sharing of ideas, concepts, and religious practices. Is it mere coincidence that the God Moses encounters is that of Abraham, an ancestor he shares with these descendants of Midian, Abraham's son by his marriage to Keturah after the death of Sarah? Indeed, how is it that Moses needs to learn from his Midianite wife that their son needs to be circumcised and how exactly to perform that significant act? (4:24-25)

Many of these same themes are picked up in our parashah. Once again Moses and Jethro are at a mountain holy to the Midianites, Sinai being the Horeb of the burning bush encounter. Once again Jethro is a font of survival information and parental advice, this time in setting up a system of judicial decision-making superior to that which Moses may have modeled on the top-down system of Egyptian tyranny. But even more significant, and surprising, is the suggestion that Jethro and Moses now share a perception of God and how that God is to be worshipped.

> Jethro rejoiced for all the good that Adonai had done to Israel, in delivering them from the Egyptians. Jethro said, "Blessed be Adonai, who has delivered you from the Egyptians and from Pharaoh. Now I know that Adonai is greater than all gods, because he delivered the people from the Egyptians, when they dealt arrogantly with them." And Jethro, Moses' father-in-law, brought a burnt offering and sacrifices to God, and Aaron came with all the elders of Israel to eat bread with Moses' father-in-law in the presence of God.
>
> (18:9-12)

The God language and the ritual elements Jethro uses here are those we have come to associate with Moses' Israelite religion, though that assumption raises a number of questions. Where would Moses have gotten his theological views and religious practices in the first place, assuming that the religious slate upon which the Israelites write is not a tabula rasa? Within Torah's chronology, there could have been some borrowing from the Egyptian world with which Prince Moses would have been familiar. But his long-standing and close relationship with a Midianite priest and the nomadic Midianites could certainly be seen as a major source upon which the Israelites could draw in the long journey to an ultimately unique monotheistic tradition.

For example, note that referring to God as Adonai, as Jethro does here, is only used in Exodus after Moses becomes part of Jethro's encampment. This, in turn, raises a challenging question. Is Jethro here conforming to Moses' theology and sacrificial practices, or might it possibly be the other way around?

In Numbers we have Moses' final meeting with Jethro, which again suggests the Midianites' role as desert mavens and resources for Israelite wilderness travel.

> Moses said to Hobab (that is, Jethro) son of Reuel the Midianite, Moses' father-in-law, "We are setting out for the place of which Adonai said, 'I will give it to you'; come with us, and we will treat you well, for Adonai has promised good to Israel."
>
> But (Jethro) said to (Moses), "I will not go; I will go back to my own land and to my kindred."
>
> (Moses) said, "Do not leave us, for you know where we should camp in the wilderness, and you will serve as eyes for us. Moreover, if you go with us, whatever good Adonai does for us, the same we will do for you." So, they set out from the mount of Adonai three days' journey with the ark of the covenant of Adonai going before them three days' journey, to seek out a resting place for

them, the cloud of Adonai being over them by day when they set out from the camp.

(Numbers 10:29-34)

Out of nowhere, it seems, Moses speaks to Jethro as if he has been with him all along. This would have Jethro present and perhaps guiding the Israelites in the construction of a holy tent of meeting, a portable sacred space appropriate for those who wander in the wilderness. Additionally, the ritual requirements of Passover, including the sacrifice of a lamb and the baking of matzot, a "bread" that would not spoil in a desert environment, might well reflect pastoral nomadic traditions and, possibly, a Midianite model. The transformation of a simple tent into a prototype for the mikdash/temple in Jerusalem, and Passover's pastoral ritual into one commemorating an exodus from Egypt would likely come much later. Finally, it is unclear whether the phrase "they set out from the mount" is meant to include Jethro's and the Midianites ongoing presence and influence, possibly manifest in mitzvot yet to be revealed in the wilderness.

At any rate, Israel seems to have contact with Midianites from the very beginning of the forty-year Israelite journey until its very end in Moab, where, shades of Moses' marriage with Zipporah, the Israelite Zimri, and the Midianite woman Cozbi present themselves before Moses in a manner that suggests their desire for an intertribal marriage. Only there, what was once acceptable is no longer even tolerated. They are killed and the Midianites are subsequently massacred, suggesting a need to radically separate peoples who were once so close to one another.

It is interesting to note that Torah seems to have a positive view of this non-Israelite priest, even though he promoted a type of intermarriage that would later be unacceptable. He is lauded in the rabbinic midrashic tradition as one who went to live in the desert primarily to study the Torah and the Jewish laws he is said to love. And his coming to Moses for conversion to Judaism explains, the rabbis might suggest, the God language and participation in a sacrificial meal of our parashah.

That non-Israelites such as Jethro, Pharaoh's daughter, and the Egyptian midwives might have supported and even saved Israelite or Hebrew lives did not seem credible to them.

But Torah clearly presents a different perspective on the matter, indicating that Jethro was an essential ingredient in the Israelite negotiation of the wilderness and its challenges, and in preparing Moses for his leadership in that undertaking. Indeed, the Israelite and Midianite people seem to share affinities in their religious outlook and practices—affinities that are later denied in Jewish tradition and, finally, rejected. For scholars and archaeologists, however, this would seem to be especially the case with Canaanites, including the Israelite appropriation of the Canaanite sacrificial system. But the particular appreciation of Jethro and his actions in support of Moses and the Israelites is clearly present in both Torah and its rabbinic commentaries.

In a way that Torah and Jewish tradition does not openly acknowledge, Jethro is the sine qua non of the Israelite liberation and wilderness experience; without him Moses would be, metaphorically and quite literally—lost. And we can only speculate about Midianite contributions and those of other people to those religious developments presented in Torah as uniquely Israelite as, for example, the practice of circumcision, attributed, as we have seen, to Jethro's daughter Zipporah.

In this sense, naming the parashah in which we find the Ten Commandments as parashat Yitro/Jethro seems entirely appropriate—honoring a wise, knowledgeable, caring, and spiritually attuned figure who we might otherwise be tempted to overlook as an unimportant "other."

Was That Golden Calf So Bad?

Torah and Jewish tradition have long castigated the worshippers of a golden calf in the Israelite wilderness as idolators, deserving punishment by God and humans. Could it be, however, that these "idol worshippers" were really true believers in the one God and their only "sin" was to oppose the priestly hierarchy and to personalize their worship experience? Beware, our portion teaches, of those who claim to punish in God's name, even if they do so with the consent of their political and religious leaders. The main events take place in Exodus 32; the revisionist view of Deuteronomy 9 tells a very different story.

Parashat Ki Tisa

Here's a shock: Those calf-worshipping Israelites may not have been as sinful as we've assumed from most common retellings of this story—including those in Hollywood epics. How can that be? The complex nature of what unfolded requires careful rereading of more than one passage.

Let's start with this text from Exodus:

> When the people saw that Moses delayed to come down from the mountain, the people gathered around Aaron and said to him, "Come, make gods (or Elohim, God) for us, who shall go before us; as for this Moses, the man who brought us up out of the land of Egypt, we do not know what has become of him."
>
> (Exodus 32:1)

In Torah's chronology, the people last saw Moses almost six weeks previously as he disappeared into "a consuming fire" at the top of Mount Sinai. (24:17-18) Had he gotten so close to God that he was consumed by holy flames and was dead? Had he become so transfixed by the divine presence that he forgot his responsibilities to the people? Were these Israelites now waiting for Moses in vain? So, they turn to Aaron, he who would soon be ordained for priestly service at the holy tabernacle, the mishkan.

While the exact nature of the people's sin has long been parsed by scholars and debated by rabbinic commentators, the nature of Aaron's actions and perhaps his sins as well seem clear:

> Aaron said to them, "Take off the gold rings that are on the ears of your wives, your sons, and your daughters and bring them to me." So all the people took off the gold rings from their ears and brought them to Aaron. He took these from them, formed them in a mold, and cast an image of a calf, and they said, "These are your gods, (or, this is your God) O Israel, who brought you up out of the land of Egypt!"
>
> (32:2-4)

It is surely no coincidence that the instructions in previous chapters for collecting gifts of gold and other precious materials from the people for the construction of the mishkan, the wilderness tabernacle, are now mirrored in the construction of the golden bull-calf. Nor does it seem happenstance that two golden cherubim are to be built and placed poised above the mishkan's gold-encrusted ark. For it is from between these two cherubim that God will, it is said, issue commandments. (25:22) Finally, the ordination ceremony of Aaron as the high priest who will serve at the mishkan would require him to lay his hands on a bull-calf, of all things, and slaughter it before Adonai, at the entrance of the Tent of Meeting. (Exod. 29:10-12; Leviticus 9:2) All of these commands now appear to be reenacted in the making of the golden or molten bull-calf, with Aaron presiding over them as its priest.

So much for the rabbis' view that the building of the mishkan is, somehow, a response to the people's sin of the golden bull-calf, so that their urge to commit idolatry might be controlled. It rather seems that the command to build the mishkan provides a precedent for Aaron to follow. Indeed, some suggest that the difference between the legitimate golden cherubim above a golden ark and Aaron's "idolatrous" golden bull-calf is only a matter of one said (by the priesthood, of course) to be commanded by God and not the other—thus a matter of hierarchical control over Israelite religion. In this sense, the term "idol" or "idolatry" is a matter of subjective definition, laying a possible claim to the idea that it might in fact be the gold calf that is religiously legitimate and not the mishkan (or even the subsequent Temple in Jerusalem). And it is in this regard that we have comments of people like Rabbi Meir Simchah Cohen (1842-1926) in his Torah commentary Meshech Hochmah "All holy things—the land of Israel, Jerusalem, the Temple Mount, the tablets—are not intrinsically holy, and they are not sanctified except by the performance of the mitzvot ... [therefore] do not imagine that the Tabernacle and the Temple are things holy unto themselves." This is an important cautionary note that we've already explored in Chapter 6, Seduction of the 'Sacred.'

Then, upon the completion of the calf, we read:

> When Aaron saw this, he built an altar before it, and Aaron made a proclamation and said, "Tomorrow shall be a festival to Adonai." They rose early the next day and offered burnt offerings and brought sacrifices of well-being, and the people sat down to eat and drink and rose up to revel.
>
> (32:5-6)

It is Aaron who makes the bull-calf, which, of course, echoes the bull-calf of his ordination ceremony; it is Aaron who builds the sacrificial altar; and it is Aaron who declares a festival to the Israelite God Adonai, while the Israelites contribute "burnt offerings" and "sacrifices of well-being," the same offerings that are to accompany the dedication of the mishkan later in Leviticus. (9:22) It seems as if Aaron has empathy for the people and willingly collaborates with them in constructing a popular version of the priestly mishkan, one that will allow the common folk contact with God that does not need to be mediated through Moses and the priests.

This, then, would be what the people mean by saying to Aaron: "Make gods (or God) for us who shall go before us." That is: Give us direct access to God as we make our way through the wilderness. And Aaron does just that. Indeed, it is most likely Aaron and not (as the usual translations have it) the people who make the declaration: "This is your god, O Israel ..." For that is what makes sense in our context, and that is what is preserved in the Greek Bible, the Septuagint. So, it is Aaron, in his priestly role, who now assures the people that their offerings at this altar will allow them to be in the presence of Adonai their liberating God.

No wonder the people are so eager to rise early in the morning to joyously celebrate a festival to Adonai, the one God, their doing so with food, drink, and dancing a manifestation, perhaps, of popular religious enthusiasm. It is a grievous mistake, however, to assume that such behavior is idolatrous.

Into this situation comes Moses. Having convinced God not to rage against the Israelites and not to punish them for their behavior, Moses proceeds to do both:

> As soon as he came near the camp and saw the calf and the dancing, Moses' anger burned hot, and he threw the tablets from his hands and broke them at the foot of the mountain. He took the calf that they had made, burned it with fire, ground it to powder, scattered it on the water, and made the Israelites drink it.
>
> (32:19-20)

Moses, it seems, is both offended by the people's lack of trust in him, and threatened by his lack of control over their religious expression. In a rage, he destroys the tablets, the work of God, depriving the people and himself of holy commandments. Then he destroys the molten bull-calf, compelling the people to drink of its powdered remains.

Without explanation, this ritual seems bizarre, though the rite of ordeal in Numbers 5 of the woman suspected of adultery, without any proof other than her husband's jealousy, can help us understand our text. If the accused wife drinks of the "waters of bitterness" without any physical suffering, she is presumed to be innocent of the charge. Since the people in our parashah drink of the golden brew without any mention of subsequent harm, the charge of idolatry would seem unwarranted.

At this point, having suffered Moses' destructive rage, a humiliating rite of ordeal, and, as we shall see, Aaron's denial of responsibility for building the calf, the people are understandably rebellious, moving Moses to impose order by force. For this he calls upon his own tribal members, the Levites, who, coincidently, are the first ones to volunteer for the task.

> He said to them, "Thus says Adonai, the God of Israel: Put your sword on your side, each of you! Go back and forth from gate to gate throughout the camp, and each of you kill your brother, your friend, and your neighbor." The sons of Levi did as Moses commanded, and about three thousand of the people fell on that day.
>
> (32:27-28)

I think it is clear here that Moses' supposed divine authorization for this attack is a complete fabrication, perhaps because Moses fears that his own weakened authority would be an insufficient motivation for such a murderous deed. From what we know of the Levites, their willingness to carry out such an act should not be surprising.

In Genesis, the Levite patriarch, Levi, along with his brother Simeon acting on their own authority, as Moses does here, took revenge against those in the city of Shechem for the perceived dishonoring of their sister, Dinah—the tragedy we read about in Chapter 8, The Silencing of Dinah.

Later, in blessing his children at the end of Genesis, Jacob declares:

> "Simeon and Levi are brothers; weapons of violence are their swords. May I never come into their council; may I not be joined to their company, for in their anger they killed men, and at their whim they maim an ox. Cursed be their anger, for it is fierce, and their wrath, for it is cruel!"
>
> (Genesis 49:5-7)

Finally, in Numbers 25 it is the zealous Pinchas, a priest and therefore a descendent of Levi, who, on his own authority, kills the intertribal lovers Zimri (of the tribe of Simeon, ironically) and Cozbi as they stand before Moses and the Israelite community. There seems to be a bloodlust at least among some Levites that leads to such a horrific murder of their own siblings, neighbors, and kin. The reason why some are killed and not others is left to the imagination of rabbinic commentators.

It is fascinating, in this regard, to note how the artist Shmuel Bak vividly portrays our Torah text in his diptych entitled, "Thou Shalt Not Kill." One panel of this work depicts the two tablets of the law falling from Moses' hands, while the other panel has the tablets lying shattered on the ground, the two Hebrew words lo tirtzach ("don't kill,") disconnected from one another so that in the background is the lo (don't), while in the foreground, repeated three times, are the words: tirtzach tirtzach tirtzach ("kill, kill, kill"). In shattering the tablets, Moses has shattered a divinely commanded moral restraint upon himself as well as upon the Levites.

Meanwhile, Aaron is fearful of repercussions for aiding the people and falsely claims that they are a people "bent on evil," then denies responsibility for making the molten figure: "So I said to them, 'Whoever has gold, take it off'; so they gave it to me, and I threw it into the fire, and out came this calf!" (Exod. 32:24) With the prospect of violence, however, he silently withdraws, abandoning the people to the Levites, who really are the ones "bent on evil." Aaron the priest might serve well as a religious leader, but he is hardly a moral one.

Moses' subsequent report of the golden bull-calf episode in Deuteronomy, however, is a revisionist view of our parashah. In addressing Israelites at the end of forty wilderness years, he claims:

> "So, I turned and went down from the mountain, while the mountain was ablaze; the two tablets of the covenant were in my two hands. Then I saw that you had indeed sinned against Adonai your God, by casting for yourselves an image; you had been quick to turn from the way that the Lord had commanded you. So, I took hold of the two tablets and flung them from my two hands, smashing them before your eyes. Then I lay prostrate before Adonai as before, forty days and forty nights; I neither

ate bread nor drank water because of all the sin you had committed, provoking Adonai by doing what was evil in his sight ... Then I took the sinful thing you had made, the calf, and burned it with fire and crushed it, grinding it thoroughly, until it was reduced to dust, and I threw the dust into the stream that runs down the mountain."

(Deuteronomy 9:15-18, 21)

Is this evidence that Moses has a faulty memory so many years after the fact, one which absolves Aaron of a central role in the construction of the bull-calf by claiming that the Israelites themselves built it? Is this a case of convenient amnesia? Or, is this an intentional revision of what actually happened? In this new version, Moses is no longer the vengeful leader who subjects the Israelites to a humiliating rite of ordeal and orders their subsequent murder. Now, Moses casts himself as atoning for their misdeeds through fasting from food and drink for forty days. Conveniently, the omission of the Levites' role in killing the 3,000 seems to support their new role in Deuteronomy as Levitical priests who are now to officiate at holy rituals, as we read:

> Then the priests, the sons of Levi, shall come forward, for Adonai your God has chosen them to minister to him and to pronounce blessings in the name of Adonai, and by their decision all cases of dispute and assault shall be settled.

(21:5)

How ironic that these one-time purveyors of extra judicial punishment are now given the task of ruling in cases of assault!

For Deuteronomy, apparently, the idea that Moses would make crucial decisions guided by rage and personal need, would use violence to gain control of his own people—and falsely claim divine authority to do so—is both morally repugnant and religiously unacceptable. Rather than openly admitting what apparently happened and criticizing Moses, Aaron, and the Levites—Deuteronomy tries to expunge their now unacceptable behavior from the historical record.

The obvious gaps in this version of the episode of the golden bull-calf, however, call attention to themselves as if to say: What's missing here? And the answer to this question is Torah's ethical challenge: Remember what Moses, Aaron, and the Levites did, so that you never again allow your political and religious leaders to behave in such a way!

Out With the Troublemakers

Throughout my study of Torah, I raise important questions about the imposition of religious and political power over marginalized persons who are then blamed for their fate. I am especially troubled by the brief story of the deaths of Nadab and Abihu, the two elder sons of the high priest Aaron. The bizarre tale of their deaths while approaching the tabernacle's holy altar is commonly told as a fate they somehow deserved. However—what if this actually was a dreadful priestly assassination in defense of a hierarchical religious institution and its domination by those who inherited their priestly roles? Is this a warning in Torah to question the motives of entrenched leaders, even those who are said to be appointed to their positions by God?

Parashat Shemini

The entire tale of Nadab and Abihu unfolds in a mere three verses in Leviticus 10—but understanding what might actually have happened that day requires deeper study. Let's start with the passage itself.

> Now Aaron's sons Nadab and Abihu each took his censer, put fire in it, and laid incense on it, and they offered strange fire before Adonai, such as he had not commanded them. And fire came out from the presence of Adonai and consumed them, and they died before Adonai.
>
> Then Moses said to Aaron, "This is what Adonai meant when he said:

> 'Through those who are near me I will show myself holy, and before all the people I will be glorified.'"
>
> And Aaron was silent.
>
> (Leviticus 10:1-3)

Let's start with the context. When this passage comes up in our weekly cycle of Torah readings, we have spent quite a while reading portions about the mishkan (the holy Tabernacle,) the korbanot (the ritual sacrifices,) and the Kohanim (the priests) who will offer these sacrifices, especially Aaron and his sons. The climax of eight days of celebration is the joyous and awe-inspiring dedication of the mizbeach, often translated as "the sacred altar," though I agree with Martin Buber and Franz Rosenzweig's more literal and powerful translation of the Hebrew word for altar, "mizbeach," into German as Schlachtstatt—"slaughter site." In describing the awestruck reaction of the people, Leviticus 9:24 says, "Fire came out from Adonai and consumed the burnt offering and the fat on the altar, and when all the people saw it, they shouted and fell on their faces."

The tragic deaths of Nadab and Abihu follow in the next three verses, which open chapter 10. These two men become the very sacrifices they are so carefully preparing to offer. The account is so terse that generations of readers have wondered what actually happened here. Is it possible that this story is a vestige—a traumatic memory of a time of human sacrifice? Were Nadab and Abihu, holy anointed priests, chosen by God to be burnt up as glorious sacrificial lambs—as Rashi and some other commentators have suggested?

Does Torah affirm this by the verse: "This is what Adonai meant when he said, 'Through those who are near me I will show myself holy, and before all the people I will be glorified?'"

Is there a clue to their fate in the inheritance pattern in Genesis that favors younger siblings? Nadab and Abihu were Aaron's oldest sons. Are their two younger brothers lurking somewhere in the altar's shadow conniving for advancement in the priestly ranks?

There is a lot more about these mysterious deaths that doesn't make sense. Nadab and Abihu were trained to perform these ritual actions before the altar, presumably in a safe and correct way. They had carefully placed burning coals and incense in their fire pans—but what was the source of this unexpected ignition? How does a panful of coals and incense suddenly burst forth with a flame of such magnitude and intensity that they are consumed, "eaten up" as the Hebrew says, by a fire said to come from God? But could there have been another, more human, source of that consuming flame?

To consider this possibility, we need to pursue at least one other clue. The description of the fire they offer is variously translated as "strange," "foreign," or "alien"—a kind of fire which, it is said, "God had not commanded them." Is this an intentional act of "estrangement" or "alienation" by these priests? Are they implicitly and publicly declaring their reservations about or even rejection of the priestly hierarchy and the institutionalized sacrificial system that they see as humanly constructed and not divine? Might we declare them in favor of a more spiritually spontaneous approach to religious practice? Are Nadab and Abihu rebels with a progressive cause? Are we then really talking here about a divinely instigated incineration, or might this rather be a more nefarious act of assassination by their fellow priests?

A helpful clue comes from Numbers 16 where we read of the punishment of the notoriously rebellious Korach and his followers. In it we find almost the exact same language that we find in our parashah:

> So each man took his censer, and they put fire in the censers and laid incense on them, and they stood at the entrance of the tent of meeting with Moses and Aaron ... And fire came out from Adonai and consumed the two hundred fifty men offering the incense.
>
> (18, 35)

Korach dares to question the divine right of Moses to rule the people, and of Aaron and the priests to have exclusive access to the most holy places. Such a threat to political and religious stability could not, apparently, be tolerated. As with Torah's command that a rebellious child be punished by death (Deuteronomy 21), so here Korach and his followers—rebellious children that they are said to be—must be similarly punished. Does this suggest that Nadab and Abihu were also seen as rebelling against the religious establishment, a threat of particular severity given their priestly status and the danger that their behavior might influence others? In both cases is rebellion actually meted out, not by God—but by priestly zealots who we know were talented in setting fire to animal flesh on the sacred altar?

As with other troubling Biblical stories we have looked at, rabbinic and other commentators tend to blame marginal characters such as Nadab and Abihu for their own suffering or, in this case, their deaths. God is justified, it is claimed, in punishing them, for surely they must have approached the altar while inebriated, or acting in ways inappropriate for priests, or blatantly defying God's commandments, each of which, they say, is supported by "proof texts" from a divinely revealed Torah. So we can just imagine how such an understanding of the "strange fire" that Nadab and Abihu bring to the altar can later be used as a biblical battering ram by those who feel a need, or even commanded, to defend traditional norms and hierarchies against innovations in religious thinking and behavior.

We are, I think, hardly surprised to find these tensions along intergenerational lines in which, as Martin Buber in *On Judaism* observes, a rigid, tradition-bound, and uncreative religion "induces fathers to reject their sons, who will not let their fathers' God be forced upon them." However, a more creative and flexible religion, which he calls religiosity, "induces sons who want to find their own God, to rebel against their fathers."

So—contrary to a more literal reading of our parashah and the concerted effort of generation upon generation of rabbinic commentators—we do well to reject the victimization of Nadab and Abihu as sinners deserving to die. Rather, with Buber in mind, we may see in their actions an intentional rebellion against their father's spiritually unsatisfying religion and a challenge to a theology that projects God as the source of a humanly constructed priestly institution. The powers that be see this as a threat that needs to be completely burned away, no matter the immorality of such an action.

Thus, Micah brings prophetic rage to bear on the immoral religious leaders of his time and place, though he could, as well, have been addressing the priests in our parashah: "Listen, you heads of Jacob and rulers of the house of Israel! Should you not know justice—you who hate the good and love the evil?"

Therefore, Micah proclaims, metaphorically perhaps, but with the same Hebrew words ascribed to the deaths of Nadab and Abihu, "You eat the flesh of my people, flay their skin off them." (3:3)

So, in the name of God, Micah demands of the House of Israel and of all the generations that follow:

> "Do justice, love kindness, and walk humbly with your God."

> (6:8)

Our Inherited Moral Dilemmas

The story of the man who gathers wood on Shabbat and is thus said to violate the proscription against work on that holy day is a frightening example of religiously sanctioned killing in violation, I believe, of the Torah's own laws. The same, I point out, is so with the man said to blaspheme God. The surprising facilitators of what might be considered "mob rule" are none other than Moses and Aaron. Do they later suffer the consequences for their unjust actions? We start with the tale of the Shabbat wood-gatherer in Numbers 15 and then reach back to a parallel text in Leviticus 24 to further emphasize our understanding of what Torah is really saying about injustice and the role of Moses and Aaron in allowing that to happen.

Parashat Shelach-Lecha

At the very end of today's parashah, Shelach-Lecha, we find an extraordinary text:

> When the Israelites were in the wilderness, they found a man gathering sticks on the Sabbath day. Those who found him gathering sticks brought him to Moses, Aaron, and the whole congregation. They put him in custody because it was not clear what should be done to him. Then Adonai said to Moses, "The man shall be put to death; all the congregation shall stone him outside the camp." The whole congregation brought him outside the camp and stoned him to death, just as Adonai had commanded Moses.
>
> (Numbers 15:32-36)

This terse narrative raises so many questions! Who was this anonymous man? How is it that some Israelites just happened to come upon him? Why was he gathering wood on Shabbat in the first place? Would he not have known that such an act was prohibited? Had he been warned of the consequences of his behavior by those who came upon him?

What particularly needs explaining, however, is the claim that "it was not clear what should be done to him." In fact, Torah does not clearly define those actions that comprise work prohibited on Shabbat, with the possible exception of lighting fire. (Exodus 35:3) So—not only would Moses and Aaron not know the punishment for wood-gathering—they, and the people as well, would not have known that it was even considered a type of prohibited work. The command that the wood-gatherer be punished by stoning for this act seems arbitrary at best, and unjust at worst.

There are readily available guidelines in Torah for determining the appropriate punishment for violations of commandments such as those pertaining to Shabbat. Indeed, such rules are clearly spelled out in our parashah in the verses immediately preceding the tale of the wood-gatherer, as if to set the stage for judging his behavior. Here it is explicitly stated that violations of God's commandments require a determination of intent. We are told:

> An individual who sins unintentionally shall present a female goat a year old for a purification offering. And the priest shall make atonement before Adonai for the one who commits an error, when it is unintentional, to make atonement for the person, who then shall be forgiven. For both the native among the Israelites and the alien residing among you, you shall have the same law for anyone who acts in error. But whoever acts high-handedly, whether native-born or an alien, affronts Adonai and shall be cut off from among the people. Because of having despised the word of Adonai and broken his commandment, such a person shall be utterly cut off and bear the guilt.

(Numbers 15:27-31)

If the wood-gatherer had not intended to violate a Shabbat prohibition, his punishment would be the offering of a she-goat, that expiation might be made for his sin and that his community would forgive him for his unintentional misdeed. However, if his was an intentional violation of God's commandment that work not be done on Shabbat, punishment would be in God's hands alone. "Such a person shall be utterly cut off (from his people) and bear the guilt." In other words, that guilt cannot be atoned for and must be borne. While the exact meaning of karait (being cut off) is not spelled out here, elsewhere, as with the punishment of being "cut off from Israel" for the sin of eating leavened bread during Passover (Exodus 12:15), there is the suggestion of social ostracism or even excommunication, a consequence far from that of capital punishment.

Why, then, did Moses and Aaron not know the correct punishment in this case? And contrary to these guidelines about intent, how is it that we have a divine decree that the man should be stoned to death? Indeed, how is it that two diametrically opposed punishments are not only found in Torah but in the same parashah, with both claiming ultimate authority?

A verse in Exodus about the profanation of Shabbat seems to address this issue. It is an example of what scholars like Ben Sommer in *Revelation and Authority* call "inner biblical exegesis," where one part of the Tanakh interprets or even disagrees with another part, though here that "exegesis" is found within a single verse:

> You shall keep the Sabbath, because it is holy for you; everyone who profanes it shall be put to death; whoever does any work on it shall be cut off from among the people.
>
> (31:14)

The first part of the verse seems to support punishment by stoning for the wood-gatherer. The second part of the verse seems to support the punishment of karait using the exact same language found in our parashah.

There are two ways of looking at this. On the one hand, we might have here an example of inner biblical interpretation: While this text does mention death for a Shabbat violator, it then defines this "death" as a metaphoric one. A more accurate reading of the verse would then be: "Everyone who profanes the Sabbath shall be put to death, [meaning] whoever does any work on it shall be cut off from among the people" that is, metaphorically "dead" to the community, the punishment of karait. On the other hand, we might have two very different voices here, one disagreeing with the other, much as we later have in Talmudic debate. There the majority view might be declared halachah (Jewish law), but the minority position is none the less preserved in the sacred text, as might be the case in this text.

A particularly clear example of Torah positions in disagreement with one another is found in the Leviticus narrative of the blasphemer, as we read:

> A man whose mother was an Israelite and whose father was an Egyptian came out among the Israelites, and the Israelite woman's son and a certain Israelite began fighting in the camp. The Israelite woman's son blasphemed the Name in a curse. And they brought him to Moses. Now, his mother's name was Shelomith daughter of Dibri, of the tribe of Dan. And they put him in custody, until the decision of Adonai should be made clear to them. Adonai spoke to Moses, saying, "Take the blasphemer outside the camp, and let all who were within hearing lay their hands on his head, and let the whole congregation stone him."
>
> (Leviticus 24:10-14)

Aside from the obvious similarity to the narrative of the woodgatherer, the sinner is now identified as the son of a mixed marriage, as if that had something to do with his being placed in custody. The punishment is the same, however—stoning by divine decree. But what follows takes this matter in a challenging direction, for God presents two very different commandments, one right after the other. First we have:

> And speak to the Israelites, saying: Anyone who curses God shall incur guilt. One who blasphemes the name of Adonai shall be put to death; the whole congregation

shall stone the blasphemer. Aliens as well as the native-born, when they blaspheme the Name, shall be put to death.

(24:15-16)

Which, however, is immediately followed—and countered—by the verse:

"Anyone who kills a human being shall be put to death."

(24:17)

And this in turn is followed by the talion law, commonly referred to as "an eye for an eye":

Anyone who kills an animal shall make restitution for it, life for life. Anyone who maims another shall suffer the same injury in return: fracture for fracture, eye for eye, tooth for tooth; the injury inflicted is the injury to be suffered. One who kills an animal shall make restitution for it, but one who kills a human being shall be put to death.

(24:18-21)

Capital punishment, that is "life for life," is here limited to cases of manslaughter or murder. Ironically then, those who stone to death the blasphemer would, it seems, be violating this commandment and thus be guilty of committing a capital offense, perhaps to die themselves by stoning. But what we might call the majority position in this debate wins the day, as we then read:

They took the blasphemer outside the camp and stoned him to death. The Israelites did as Adonai had commanded Moses.

(24:23)

As with the case of the wood-gatherer and the law in Exodus for one who profanes Shabbat, the blasphemer narrative presents opposing arguments on capital punishment—one for stoning and one very much against it—almost as if they are in direct conversation with one another.

So, how are we to understand the pivotal role that Moses and Aaron play in these narratives when they appeal to God for a judicial ruling, what would later be called a pesak din, a legal decision by the rabbis? We have already questioned why Moses and Aaron do not seem to know the correct punishment. But what if they already knew that there were two possible punishments for the transgressor? What if they were unable or unwilling to decide which they should opt for—to stone or not to stone? Would they have feared that not all commandments in Torah are from God and that the command for stoning might have come from a human agency—perhaps from those who just happened to come upon the wood-gatherer or those who claimed to hear the half-Israelite utter words said to be blaspheming God?

A courageous display of leadership at this point would have demanded a determination of the sinner's intent, questioned the reliability of witnesses, and quite possibly have challenged the morality of punishment by stoning to death. But Moses and Aaron are not such leaders—at least not here. They seem to be facing an implicit challenge to their leadership and, as a result, they accede to the call to kill, whether that call is truly a divine commandment, or merely the chanting of a mob for blood.

Reading Torah through the lens of medieval commentators such as Rashi and Ibn Ezra can be helpful in surfacing problems with biblical texts, though they often seem more interested in justifying the actions of leaders such as Moses and Aaron than in critiquing them. What is more helpful, however, is the rabbinic determination that the necessary conditions for stoning in the case of the rebellious child (Deuteronomy 21:18-21) are so difficult to meet as to prevent it from ever happening, with the implication that capital punishment for any reason is unacceptable.

While the rabbinic commentators are often inclined to use their considerable interpretive skills to harmonize contradictory Torah texts, I have yet to find such effort applied to the obviously different punishment guidelines for the blasphemer, the wood-gatherer, and the one who profanes Shabbat.

Could it be that in doing so our sages would need to address the difficult issue of contradictory commandments attributed to God, a minefield they might be reluctant to enter?

I would rather think that, in their wisdom, the rabbis (and perhaps the editors of Torah) concluded that leaving such contradictions unresolved would be the best way to engage future readers, students, and religious communities in an ongoing dialogue with Torah. Even more importantly, perhaps, in the way we live our spiritual and religious lives, is the reality that we have inherited this struggle with the moral legitimacy of capital punishment and the ongoing debate about what circumstances, if any, we would countenance the taking of a human life.

So, Who Gets to Be a Prophet?

> *Balaam is one of my favorite biblical characters, in spite of Torah's attempts to question his validity as a true prophet of God who firmly embraces the Israelite tradition and who teaches it through the compelling poetry of his oracles. He is the target of religious bias and suspicion and ultimately pays with his life for his courageous actions in blessing Israelites. Along with Pharaoh's daughter and, as we shall see later on, with the sailors who tried to save Jonah's life—Balaam might better be recognized as a "righteous one among the nations." Make up your own mind by carefully following his poetry in Numbers 23 and 24.*

Parashat Balak

Our Torah portion for this Shabbat, parashat Balak, is a strange one, and Balaam son of Beor, its main character, is one of Torah's more interesting figures. At first presented as a Mesopotamian wizard, by the end of the parashah Balaam seems more like an Israelite, and a prophetic one at that. Paying close attention to the words attributed to Balaam will, I think, allow us to affirm this. We will, along the way, be treated to beautiful poetry, particularly evident in the original Hebrew.

But Balaam, who so clearly and wonderfully blesses Israelites and disobeys a royal command to curse them, is subsequently condemned as an idolator (Numbers 31:16), justly deserving assassination by zealous Israelite priests in a later passage. This is a complex story with many nuances. In Deuteronomy 23:5-6, Joshua 24:9-10, and Nehemiah 13:2, it is confidently stated that Balaam really wanted to curse Israel, but was coerced by God into blessing them. Balaam also is widely defamed in rabbinic literature as a false and evil prophet.

However, I think our careful reading of these texts reveals him to be a prophet who is both true and righteous.

So, why does our biblical and post-biblical tradition have such a difficulty seeing this outsider as a genuine prophet and righteous gentile—or at least a praiseworthy figure—who courageously choses to bless Israel against all the pressures and inducements to do otherwise?

In our parashah, the Israelites are passing through the territory of Moab at the very end of their forty-year wilderness journey. The Moabite king, Balak, sends messengers to far-off Mesopotamia, to convince Balaam, a kosem, or diviner, as he is called in Joshua (3:22), to come and curse the Israelites, that he may defeat them in battle. But Israel's final encounter with a people standing between them and Canaan is to be a peaceful one, thanks to the power of Balaam's daring and wonderfully creative words of blessing, words that he claims God put into his mouth.

If we really want to know Balaam, we need to look closely at his oracles and not be misled by what others say about him, or distracted, as so many seem to be, by the parashah's tale of a talking ass.

> Then Balaam uttered his (first) oracle, saying:
>
> "Balak has brought me from Aram,
>
> the king of Moab from the eastern mountains:
>
> 'Come, curse Jacob for me.
>
> Come, denounce Israel!'"
>
> (Numbers 23:7)

Balaam's poetry is lean and beautiful, and its use of parallel phrases that echo and expand one another is similar to Jacob's farewell words to his sons in Genesis 49 and to Moses' song to the Israelites in Deuteronomy 33. It is, as well, interesting to note that the ancient Hebrew vocabulary our poet employs suggests that his oracle is older than the prose context within which it is embedded. So much for commentators who pay closer attention to what is likely later narrative material in their efforts to depreciate Balaam and his intentions toward the Israelites!

The story with which the parashah begins is summarized here, but with a significant difference. Balak had objectified the Israelites as "this horde" and "this people" that is like "an ox licking up grass."

Balaam knows who they really are: Jacob and Israel. And he further knows this truth:

> How can I curse whom God has not cursed?
>
> How can I denounce those whom Adonai has not denounced?
>
> ... Who can count the dust of Jacob
>
> or number the dust cloud of Israel?
>
> (Numbers 23:8, 10)

Here Balaam asserts that the Israelites have realized God's promise to Abram in Genesis: "I will make your offspring like the dust of the earth, so that if one can count the dust of the earth, your offspring also can be counted." (Genesis 13:16) Not only is Balaam familiar with Israel's ancestral narrative, he also affirms their covenantal relationship with their God, Adonai. Then he claims affinity with Israel by ending this first oracle with what sounds like a statement of commitment to their well-being:

> Let me die the death of the upright,
>
> and let my end be like his!
>
> (Numbers 23:10)

Here, of course, we have an echo of Ruth's declaration of loyalty to Naomi and her people: "Where you die, I will die, and there will I be buried ..." (Ruth 1:17)

In the second oracle Balaam informs Balak, his erstwhile sponsor, that not only can he not curse Israel, but that he must bless them, as he says: "(God) has blessed, and I cannot revoke it." (Numbers 23:20) After which this diviner ironically acknowledges that: "Surely there is no enchantment against Jacob, no divination against Israel." (23:23)

So Balaam, in blessing Jacob and Israel, cannot, by this definition, really be a diviner, but rather, within the purview of the Israelite world, he is a prophet. Whereupon Balaam continues his oracle with words of praise:

> (Israel is) a people rising up like a lioness
>
> and rousing itself like a lion!
>
> (23:24)

If Balaam channeled God's blessing of Abram in the first oracle, he now uses the same language that Jacob uses in blessing Judah at the end of Bere'shit:

> "Judah is a lion's whelp; from the prey, my son, you have gone up. He crouches down, he stretches out like a lion, like a lioness—who dares rouse him up?"
>
> (Genesis 49:9)

It is, however, when we get to the third oracle that Balaam really sounds like a prophet of Israel. In noting that "the spirit of God came upon him," Balaam proclaims:

> The oracle of one who hears the words of God,
>
> who sees the vision of Shadai, the Almighty,
>
> who falls down but with eyes uncovered.
>
> (Numbers 24:4)

Having previously spoken of the divine as God and Adonai, he now uses the more sparsely employed Shadai, Almighty, identifying himself as one who sees "the vision of the Almighty." By definition, then, Balaam is a hozeh, one who has revelatory visions, who hears God's speech and prostrates himself as one in a trance, all of which reminds us of such prophets as Ezekiel (1:28), Jeremiah (7:13), and Amos (7:16). This oracle ends with words of Isaac's blessing of Jacob (Genesis 27:29) with only a slight reversal of word order:

> Blessed is everyone who blesses you,
>
> and cursed is everyone who curses you!

(Numbers 24:9)

In the context of Balaam's narrative, this implies that he, in blessing Israel, is blessed, and Balak, in calling for the curse of Israel is, ironically, the one who is cursed.

In the concluding oracle, having rejected the demand to curse Israelites, then proceeding to bless them, Balaam now describes how Israel will later defeat her enemies, including, most significantly, Moab. For this is the vision that he receives from God the Almighty One.

> I see him but not now;
>
> I behold him but not near—
>
> a star shall come out of Jacob,
>
> and a scepter shall rise out of Israel;
>
> it shall crush the foreheads of Moab
>
> and the heads of all the Shethites.

(24:17)

In this vision, Balaam anticipates the destruction of Moab described in Jeremiah's lengthy prophesy (Jeremiah 48:45) using almost the same language. He also predicts a future and eternal Israel monarchy, reflected in Jacob's blessing of Judah: "The scepter shall not depart from Judah, nor the ruler's staff from between his feet," (Genesis 49:10) for which Rambam has a messianic interpretation: "'A star rises from Jacob,' this is David; 'a scepter comes forth from Israel,' this is king messiah." (Mishneh Torah, Kings and Wars, 11)

So, finally, how do we judge Balaam? He's hardly just a Mesopotamian diviner. He's hardly one unfamiliar with Tanakh. There are parallels between him and Abram, Moses, Isaac, and Jacob. His blessings are profound and his commitment to Israel's well-being manifest. As a poet, his language is reminiscent of the Psalmist and Job. In his prophetic role, he fits in with the Nevi'im (Prophets).

Does that make him a genuine prophet of God? Quite possibly. Does that suggest that he is a closet idolator? Clearly not. In fact, if we only know Balaam through his oracles (which scholars see as the earliest core of the narrative), we might think he is a personification of the Jewish biblical experience and its poetic literature. It almost seems as if Moses and our patriarchs are present in blessing the Israelites as they are about to enter their Promised Land. Indeed, as Balaam comes from Babylonia to Moab at the border of the land of Israel, so too will the Jews much later return from Babylonian exile to Jerusalem with the Torah, "the book of the law of Moses." (Nehemiah 8:1) So we might ask, are Balaam and his oracles a prequel to that much later historical event? Is this another indication that Balaam is a true prophet of Israel?

Whether or not Balaam actually existed, our parashah presents us with the wonderfully challenging truth that a stranger who comes from afar might, ironically, be the very one who brings peace and blessing to Israel in its time of need. Indeed, the more closely we listen to Balaam's words, the less strange he seems, and certainly the less deserving of the distrust and scorn he receives in the Tanach and rabbinic literature.

However, there just might be an obvious and public corrective to this misperception. For it is the chanting of one of Balaam's blessings from the Jewish prayerbook that echoes through the synagogue at the very beginning of every morning service:

> Mah tovu ohalecha ya'akov, mishkenotecha Yisrael
>
> How fair are your tents, O Jacob,
>
> your encampments, O Israel!!

(Numbers 24:5)

Star-Crossed Lovers

Cozbi and Zimri are Torah's Romeo and Juliet, she of a prominent Midianite family and he likewise of a family of status, though an Israelite one. They are, it seems, open about their relationship, only to be horribly killed for their affections. The background is the changing nature of the Israelite-Midianite relationship, to the detriment of both peoples, as we shall see. While religious zealotry prevails in this story, we continue to struggle with social and religious attitudes toward public expressions of loving relationships in our own day. Numbers 25 brings us into this moral thicket. For me, this devar Torah also has personal resonance because I delivered this reflection on the fortieth birthday of our wonderful daughter, Daniella. She first experienced the Lomdim community, with myself and my wife, just after her fourth birthday.

Parashat Pinchas

This Torah portion from Numbers flows from the portion we just explored. The Israelites are on the cusp of entering the Promised Land and we just looked at Balaam's dilemma over cursing or blessing the Israelites as they approached the territory of Moab. Then, at the end of that account, that parashah turns dark and deadly. Israelite men, said to be "whoring with the Moabite women" and making sacrifices to their god Baal are killed by their own leaders.

This, in turn, introduces us to the tale of Torah's star-crossed lovers. It is a text that I find both compelling and horrifying:

> Just then one of the Israelites came and brought a Midianite woman into his family, in the sight of Moses and in the sight of the whole congregation of the Israelites, while they were weeping at the entrance

of the tent of meeting. When Phinehas son of Eleazar, son of Aaron the priest, saw it, he got up and left the congregation. Taking a spear in his hand, he went after the Israelite man into the tent and pierced the two of them, the Israelite and the woman, through the belly. So, the plague was stopped among the Israelites.

(Numbers 25:6-8)

It is this story that is alluded to when our new parashah opens with exuberant praise for Pinchas who is promised "a covenant of perpetual priesthood, because he was zealous for his God," (25:13) which action, we now know, is the brutal killing of an Israelite man and a Midianite woman. This couple, anonymous in last week's reading, are now given names and a social status, perhaps explaining, in part, the unacceptable nature of their relationship:

The name of the slain Israelite man who was killed with the Midianite woman was Zimri son of Salu, head of an ancestral house belonging to the Simeonites. The name of the Midianite woman who was killed was Cozbi daughter of Zur, who was the head of a clan, an ancestral house in Midian.

(25:14-15)

Far from being just any Israelite and Midianite—perhaps a couple chosen at random so that such unacceptable unions be made an example in the presence of Moses and the whole Israelite community—we now realize that Cozbi and Zimri represent leading tribal families. We are told that he "brought a Midianite woman into his family," which sounds like a formal introduction, either to his lover or, more likely I think, his wife. This could even be seen as a ritual to bind their respective tribes more closely together. But the priestly class, Torah's ideological gatekeepers, would see this as a threat to Israel's separate and unique identity as an am kadosh and am segulah, God's holy and treasured people. Pinchas, the grandson of the high priest Aaron no less, takes it upon himself to mete out the violent punishment that God now praises in our parashah as righteously zealous.

Did our lovers knowingly seek to challenge the religious hierarchy and its social restrictions? Did they really think priests would value the love of a man and a woman over what they might claim to be the good of the larger community? Were Cozbi and Zimri prepared for martyrdom on behalf of their cause? These are matters of conjecture. What is not a matter of conjecture is that killing a single Midianite woman, because she is a Midianite, will prove to be a very slippery moral slope.

As a consequence of idolatrous acts in the previous parashah, along with the episode of Cozbi and Zimri, God is said to have commanded an attack on the Midianites. In a subsequent Torah portion, Mattot, that attack will escalate to an act of ethnic cleansing, a particularly abhorrent action especially since these Midianites seem to pose no physical threat to the Israelite forces. And so we read in our parashah:

> Adonai spoke to Moses, saying, "Harass the Midianites, and defeat them, for they have harassed you by the trickery with which they deceived you in the affair of Peor, and in the affair of Cozbi, the daughter of a leader of Midian, their sister; she was killed on the day of the plague that resulted from Peor."

(25:16-18)

There are three underlying themes here that come to our attention:

1. Mentioning Cozbi in the same breath as "trickery," the "affair of (the god Baal) Peor," and the "plague" that resulted, suggests that she was guilty of seducing Zimri into idolatry and so deserving of her violent end. Thus, we have the timeless ploy of blaming the victim.

2. Killing is assumed to be an appropriate weapon against unacceptable social unions in which the women are seen as the primary actors and the men passive innocents trapped and manipulated into abominable religious practices they would, it is assumed, otherwise have avoided. The trope of the dangerously

seductive gentile woman is reflected in Deuteronomy's warnings about the Canaanites and is said to necessitate their exile from the Promised Land.

3. That Midianites are charged with a collective guilt for the crimes ascribed to some of their women is here presented as an unchallenged justification for God's command to "avenge the Israelites on the Midianites," (Numbers 31:2) that is, to kill them.

In a way, it all comes back to Midianites. Cozbi, it appears, is killed not because of anything she did, but because of what she was: a Midianite. The same is true, I suggest, of the subsequent killing of Midianite men, women, and children. What we have, not coincidently, I think, is a connection with Midianites at the very beginning of Israel's forty years in the wilderness, and now at its very end.

They are, it seems, a nomadic people living in and traveling through the same lands connected with the desert wanderings of the Israelites: Sinai, Canaan, and now, the territory of Moab, East of the Dead Sea. In each of these places their presence and actions influence the Israelite narrative in profound ways.

In Canaan, Midianite traders pull Joseph from the pit and sell him into Egyptian servitude. (Genesis 37:28)

We have already explored Moses' relationship with Jethro in Chapter 11. To summarize here: In Sinai, Moses finds refuge with the Midianite priest Reual (another name for Jethro), marries his daughter Zipporah, and shepherds his flock on the holy mountain Horeb with its burning bush. (Exodus 2-3) And it is with Midianites that he spends, according to Torah's chronology, some forty years, surely an influential time in his life. The close connection Moses has with his Midianite father-in-law is further reflected at Mount Sinai where Jethro greets Moses with such words as: "Blessed be Adonai, who has delivered you from the Egyptians and from Pharaoh. Now I know that Adonai is greater than all gods." (Exodus 18:10-11) More notably, Jethro guides Moses in the necessary restructuring of his judicial system. When Moses and Israel need support and guidance, they turn to Jethro and the Midianites, intermarry with them, and share their religious beliefs and rituals. At the holy place of Sinai, Jethro brings sacrifices to the God of Moses; at the holy place of Peor, Israelite men present offerings to the god Baal.

The religious affinity between these two peoples is further affirmed at the beginning of the earlier parashah, as King Balak turns to Midianite elders to convince Balaam to curse the Israelites. But asking a Midianite to turn against Israelites with whom they are connected by history, family, and perhaps religious convictions and practices, would hardly seem a recipe for success. It should have come as no surprise that Balaam, when he finally does come to Balak, does so with God-language that both Jethro and Moses would surely recognize, referring to Adonai, God, and Shadai (the Almighty One)—and with a message that he is commanded by God not to curse the Israelites, but rather to bless them.

Balaam's efforts aside, what once seemed to be a positive relationship between these two peoples is now seen as a highly problematic one. Israel had intimate and important connections with Midianites at the outset of their forty-year journey and, on occasion, in the midst of the Sinai wilderness. Aside from sharing some religious traditions and beliefs, they had in common social structures that were minimally hierarchical and institutional. But the religion reflected in our parashah is one that has become more highly structured, controlled by the priestly cult, and clearly patriarchal, the type of institutionalization of religions over time that the sociologist Max Weber calls the "routinization of charisma."

What once was a relationship of mutuality and respect is now one of bitter contention and degradation. The priesthood now demands an Israelite identity totally separate from that of the Midianites, for these two peoples had, it seems, come to value too much of what they shared and, in doing so, overlook that which should have set them apart. So, God's command to harass and defeat the Midianites might reflect an attempt to erase a disturbing memory of how close these two people once were.

Cozbi's and Zimri's misfortune was to love one another at the wrong time and in the wrong place. The Moses at one end of the wilderness journey could indeed marry a Midianite woman and might have allowed these two to marry as well, but the Moses at the other end of the journey, as we see, could no longer condone such a union, however hypocritical such a stance might seem. These early and late versions of Moses collide in the disaster visited upon these two lovers.

However, if we pull back for a moment from the immediate situation of our Torah text, we can, perhaps, see another element contributing to Cozbi and Zimri's fate. The priest and scribe Ezra will later warn those Judean men who returned with him to Jerusalem from Babylonian exile of the dangers of intermarriage, lest their "holy seed" becomes "mixed" with that of the peoples of the land, polluting that which is holy, including the land itself that their mixed children would inherit. (Ezra 9:11-12) Holiness for Ezra is no longer dependent on moral behavior, as we read in Leviticus 19, "that you may become holy," but is, rather, an intrinsic Judean trait. Next to Israel, other peoples are now defined as "unholy," morally and religiously inferior, and "unclean," as Ezra puts it.

Is this the real backstory to the tragedy of Cozbi and Zimri, edited into our parashah many years later from a post-exilic perspective? Did they cross a line that, ultimately, had little to do with Midianites, per se, and everything to do with Cozbi not being an Israelite woman and therefore unalterably unacceptable as Zimri's wife? Indeed, their high status in their respective tribes might have dangerously supported an argument that they are, in fact, one another's equal and so could marry.

Questions of historical veracity aside, I am concerned with the values reflected in our parashah, for they condone exclusionary, deprecatory, and even violent behavior towards non-Israelites and their religious practices. They affirm an opposition to intermarriage that, as we have seen, conflates idolatry, immorality, misogyny, and a view that Israelites are intrinsically superior to other peoples.

Cozbi and Zimri are hardly well-known figures in the larger biblical and Jewish narrative. But each time I read of their plight, I am deeply moved by a love that transcends tribal identities and arbitrary proscriptions. Each time I read of their fate, I am deeply offended by Pinchas and a horrific abuse of power said to be for the glorification of God. Cozbi and Zimri are caught between two powerful and contradictory forces, one that strives to affirm life and one that seeks to extinguish its vitality. Torah preserves this tension by confronting us with the heartbreaking and morally terrifying story of Cozbi and Zimri. That, it seems to me, makes this text a timeless reminder that if we allow zealots to impose their religious convictions on others, then we court the very real danger that the forces of hatred and intolerance may prevail in our days as well.

No, *We* Are the Chosen Ones

What a Torah portion we have here! It has the second listing of Ten Commandments, biblical verses that are now part of the Jewish prayerbook, phrases that we read at the Passover Seder, and readings that reflect a positive sense of Jewish identity. Alas, this portion also contains a decidedly negative view of those who are not Israelites—an "other" as opposed to an "us"—deserving of harsh depreciation, violent repression, and, ultimately, exile, so that Israelites may enjoy sole possession of the land of the Canaanites. Harmonizing these antagonistic teachings in a way that might result in a just and empathic relationship between these two peoples is an underlying mission for Torah itself—and an ongoing one as we try to interpret Deuteronomy 5:1-7:11 within the context of our own lives.

Parashat Va-etchannan

Parashat Va-etchannan contains some of the most widely quoted sections in Torah, for in it we find:

shema yisrael—

"Hear, O Israel! Adonai is our God, Adonai alone."

(Deuteronomy 6:4)

"You shall love Adonai your god with all your heart and with all your soul and with all your might."

(6:5)

On top of that, we have a second iteration of the commandments: Do not murder, do not steal, do not covet what is not yours, etc. (5:6-18)

This text is with us any time we lift our Torah scrolls before the holy ark and say: "This is the law that Moses set before the Israelites." (4:44)

The wise child at our seder recalls this parashah with the question: "What is the meaning of the decrees and the statutes and the ordinances that Adonai our God has commanded you (for the observance of Passover)?" (6:20)

And our Passover Haggadah also draws from this parashah in proclaiming our collective experience of bondage and persecution: "We were Pharaoh's slaves in Egypt." (6:21)

Alongside the stories of our biblical patriarchs, the liberation from Egypt, and the revelation at Sinai, it is this parashah, with its theological focus and its emphasis on a mitzvah-doing way of life, that seeks to promote a unique religious identity: Believe this, teach this, do this, and you will be God's covenanted people.

But, in tension with this positive construction of Israelite identity in our parashah, there is a dark, negative side: an assertion of who and what we are not, a construction of a "them" as opposed to "us"—an "other" whose beliefs and behaviors are said to be religiously and morally abhorrent and who are thus deserving of the depreciation, persecution, and expulsion that God is said to command. They are a people, often collectively referred to as Canaanites, whose land, so our Torah says, repeatedly, was promised to our patriarchal ancestors and whose very presence is felt to be an existential threat.

We must read, then, that part of our parashah that is, perhaps, not widely quoted:

> "When Adonai your God brings you into the land that you are about to enter and occupy and he clears away many nations before you—the Hittites, the Girgashites, the Amorites, the Canaanites, the Perizzites, the Hivites, and the Jebusites, seven nations more numerous and mightier than you—and when Adonai your God gives them over to you and you defeat them, then you must utterly destroy them. Make no covenant with them and show them no mercy. Do not intermarry with them,

giving your daughters to their sons or taking their daughters for your sons, for that would turn away your children from following me, to serve other gods. Then the anger of Adonai would be kindled against you, and he would destroy you quickly. But this is how you must deal with them: break down their altars, smash their pillars, cut down their sacred poles and burn their idols with fire. For you are a people holy to Adonai your God; Adonai your God has chosen you out of all the peoples on earth to be his people, his treasured possession."

(7:1-6)

Contemporary biblical scholarship and an increasing body of archaeological evidence tell us that there was not always a clear distinction between ancient Israelites and the Canaanites among whom they lived. Indeed, the biblical presentation of their mutual antagonism most likely reflects a much later process of identity construction. The "Canaanite," depicted in Torah as an irredeemably evil promoter of infanticide and a seductive idolator bent on converting Israelite children to abhorrent religious practices and detestable moral behavior is, most likely, not objective reality—but rather a subjective literary creation. And the "Israelite," presented as intrinsically holy, a zealot bent on carrying out the commands of a singular and jealous God seems, likewise, is an ideological construct.

What troubles me about our parashah, however, is not the question of its historical veracity, but the model it presents for how Israelites, or later Judahites, or still later Jews, ought to affirm an identity as different from, even religiously and morally superior to, those it sees as "other."

I do not think we can simply skip over such passages in Torah. We need to interrogate these texts in a way that is intellectually honest, morally challenging, and consistent with a sense that Torah is, for me at least, a uniquely valuable ethical resource.

Unfortunately, I find traditional rabbinic commentaries singularly unhelpful in this effort, as they invariably affirm the evil intentions of the Canaanites and the righteousness of their dispossession by the Israelites. However, a contemporary teaching has opened up for me a whole new way of approaching such a morally troubling text. Lutheran scholar Darrell Fasching fell in love with and married a Jewish woman, an experience that, for him, demanded a radical rereading of his sacred New Testament scripture. In *Narrative Theology After Auschwitz*, Fasching approaches that text with what he calls a "decentered" theology. Before his marriage, he saw scripture through Christian eyes, identifying with Jesus and the perspective of New Testament texts that appears to depreciate the Jews.

Now he needed to shift the "center" of his concern, seeing and critiquing the text through her Jewish eyes. He does this not only to provide an empathic corrective to a one-sided narrative, but because he knows that those texts, considered by Christians to be sacred, contributed to the formation of anti-Jewish and antisemitic values and behaviors that, he argues, found their most evil expression in Nazi racial ideology.

With Fasching as my guide, I now need to radically reread my sacred scripture with a "decentered" theology, no longer identifying solely with those Israelites who seek to suppress Canaanite religious rituals, destroy their sacred sites, and violently expel them from their native land. While I acknowledge the difficulty of such an undertaking, I believe that Torah implicitly imposes upon me the task of seeing and critiquing these actions as if I were a Canaanite. What might it have felt like to be invaded by those claiming my land, my houses, my vineyards, and my crops, while declaring a divine right to do so? What might it have felt like to have my holy sites and sacred vessels pillaged and polluted by those following, they say, the will of a jealous God? What might it have felt like to have my very humanity depreciated and myself and my family subjected to hateful speech and gratuitous violence? How then—they and we might ask—could it possibly be claimed that such actions were just, and that those who performed them were a righteous, indeed the treasured, people of a merciful God?

The Jewish challenge, I suggest, is to read, and even embrace such troubling Torah texts as opportunities to develop the capacity for empathy with those our tradition sees as a "them," as a "not us," unworthy of those rights and privileges we would demand for ourselves.

It is, I think, important to remember my pointing out at the very beginning of these commentaries, that Torah, a source of mitzvot and the narrative of a chosen people, does not start with the revelation at

Sinai or the going out of Egypt, those very particularistic sources of Israelite identity, but rather with a universal, and morally compelling truth: that beyond tribal, ethnic, national, and religious divisions, all humans are created, as Torah says, b'tselem Elohim, in the image of God. (Gen. 1:27)

In this way, our tradition teaches that how we see and treat the divine image in one another, even those we regard as strangers, is either an act of respecting or defaming God, of sublime worship or abhorrent idolatry. For we surely know that all of us are fundamentally far more kin to one another than we are different, and, as our creation story would have it, each of us is of ultimate value. This teaching, this difficult, challenging but always necessary teaching is not, as our Torah says, beyond our capacity to embrace and incorporate into our individual and communal lives.

Perhaps this is why our text at the beginning of Genesis is complemented by these verses at the end of Deuteronomy, the words of Moses to the people:

> Surely, this commandment that I am commanding you today is not too hard for you, nor is it too far away. It is not in heaven, that you should say, "Who will go up to heaven for us and get it for us so that we may hear it and observe it?" Neither is it beyond the sea, that you should say, "Who will cross to the other side of the sea for us and get it for us so that we may hear it and observe it?" No, the word is very near to you; it is in your mouth and in your heart for you to observe.
>
> (Deuteronomy 30:11-14)

And in the very center of a Torah bookended by the creation of life in Genesis and the instructions for living that life in Deuteronomy is that teaching in the middle of Leviticus, in the very heart of our sacred scroll: v'ahavtah lerei'echa kamocha "Love your neighbor as yourself: I am Adonai." (Leviticus 19:18)

Or, as it was later taught in the Talmud by Rabbi Hillel: "Do not do to others what you hated when it was done to you."

So, in this one remarkable parashah, we find powerful sources of a Jewish identity—"Hear Israel"; "Love God"; "Do not murder"; "We were Pharoah's slaves in Egypt"—and, at the same time, a powerful challenge to interrogate that identity, if, as a consequence, it denies, in word and deed, the full humanity of "others," those who are not "us," even those called "Canaanites." For they are, as Leviticus says, kamocha, "just like you," made b'tselem Elohim, "in the image of God."

As our parashah declares:

> ***This*** is the law that Moses set before the Israelites.
>
> (Deuteronomy 4:4)

Scapegoating Your Enemy

The Torah verses about Amalek, Israel's archenemy, have become a part of the Jewish religious calendar. This passage is read on the Shabbat before Purim which, in turn, "announces" the coming of Passover, but one month later. And each holy day recalls an existential threat to the people of Israel by the designs of a tyrannical figure: Haman, a descendent of Amalek, on Purim; and Pharaoh on Passover. Amalek is said to have viciously fought against Israelites in the Sinai wilderness and his memory is, therefore, to be blotted out by God (or his descendants killed by Israelites). The problem for the reader of Torah, however, is one of changing times and conditions, as the once powerful Amalekites, no longer an existential threat, will be treated as if they still are. The story comes together across a number of sections of the Tanakh: starting with Exodus 17 and Deuteronomy 25, moving on to I Samuel 15, and winding up with chapters 3, 8, and 9 in the Book of Esther.

Shabbat Zachor

The maftir, the concluding Torah verses for Shabbat Zachor, starting with the word zachor (remember) bids us to remember Amalek's attack on vulnerable Israelites in the wilderness. It is, in a way, an introduction to the following week's holiday of Purim. Our reading from Deuteronomy may be a familiar text, but it is also a complicated one.

> Zachor! Remember what Amalek did to you on your journey out of Egypt, how he attacked you on the way, when you were faint and weary, and struck down all who lagged behind you; he did not fear God. Therefore, when Adonai your God has given you rest from all your

enemies on every hand, in the land that Adonai your God is giving you as an inheritance to possess, you shall blot out the remembrance of Amalek from under heaven; do not forget.

(Deuteronomy 25:17-19)

We are commanded: Zachor! Remember! But what exactly are we to remember? What happened, as it says, "on your journey out of Egypt"? The initial report of this encounter with Amelek is back in Exodus, as we read:

> Then Amalek came and fought with Israel at Rephidim ... And Joshua defeated Amalek and his people with the sword. Then Adonai said to Moses ... I will utterly blot out the memory of Amalek from under heaven ... [and] Adonai will have war with Amalek from generation to generation.
>
> (Exod. 17:8, 13-14,16)

The Amalekites may have started the fight, but, in the end, they were soundly defeated. Our maftir portion, curiously, provides a very different "memory" of what Amalek did: "He attacked you on the way, when you were faint and weary, and struck down all who lagged behind you." In the first report, Amalek boldly attacks Israel. However, in this description, there is a stealth attack on vulnerable stragglers. In the first account, Israel is powerful and victorious; in the second, "faint and weary." Does Moses have a faulty memory? Are there two different traditions at play here, one conflicting with the other? Or is there an intentional misrepresentation in Deuteronomy, one that prefers to see a vulnerable rather than powerful Israel, and one that sees Amalekites as a powerful, if loathsome people, rather than a defeated enemy?

In a way, our maftir is reminiscent of the account of the spies who scouted out the Promised Land and returned to Moses with an account reflecting low self-esteem: "the people who live in the land are giants ... and to ourselves we seemed like grasshoppers, and so we seemed to them." (Numbers 13:28, 33) Alas, they are great; we are puny.

In addition, there is a problem with the wording of our maftir text, for it can be read in two very different ways. Most English translations read something like: "Undeterred by fear of God, [Amalek] attacked you on the way, when you were faint and weary, and struck down all who lagged behind you." Even the marginally better translation we have been using ends with: "He (that is Amalek) did not fear God." Those cowardly Amalekites did not "fear God," that is, they were morally reprehensible in pouncing on those who could not defend themselves. Such actions should not be forgotten, and their perpetrators stigmatized for their immoral behavior.

But the actual word order and the grammar of the Hebrew sentence seems to say something significantly different: "[Amalek] attacked you on the way, when you were faint and weary, and struck down all who lagged behind you, and you [Israel] were not fearful of God."

In this reading, the Israelites did not "fear God," and they left the most vulnerable among the people without protection. Is this, then, what needs to be acknowledged and remembered? Do we need to remember how Israel failed to protect the vulnerable? Is the command zachor in fact a warning not to ignore the needs of the poor and needy in society, as the twentieth century Jerusalem rabbi Mordecai Yehudah Lieb Zaks suggests?

These uncertainties and contradictions aside, the memory of Amalek is to be "blotted out from under heaven," whether by God in Exodus or by the Israelites themselves in Deuteronomy. Amalek is thus one, among many, of whom Jewish tradition says yimach sh'mo v'zichro (may their name and memory be wiped out). The irony, of course, is that by remembering those whose names and memories we wish to "blot out," we keep those names and memories alive in our collective consciousness—though it is only with Amalek that we are commanded to do so.

But the terrible and much later consequence of using Amalek as a paradigm of evil unfolds in the haftarah portion for this Shabbat, as the prophet Samuel instructs King Saul:

> Thus says Adonai of hosts: I will punish the Amalekites
> for what they did in opposing the Israelites when they

came up out of Egypt. Now go and attack Amalek and utterly destroy all that they have; do not spare them, but kill both man and woman, child and infant, ox and sheep, camel and donkey.

(1 Samuel 15:2-3)

While the exact meaning of "blotting out" a memory is not spelled out in Torah, its application in the Book of Samuel is lethal: a version of "ethnic cleansing," we might say. The descendants of Amalek are held responsible for the sins of their ancestor, and their memory should be "blotted out," that is, they deserve to be killed. Samuel says this is a divine decree. So Saul unquestioningly obeys the prophet, putting all the Amalekites to the sword, but sparing the life of his fellow king, Agag. And it is for this act of disobedience that Saul must forfeit his throne.

While Saul, at least, displays a modicum of mercy in preserving the king's life, Samuel will have none of it, and, in a zealous rage, hews King Agag into pieces. I have always appreciated Martin Buber's comment on this text in *The Philosophy of Martin Buber*: "Samuel may have gotten a message from God, but he misunderstood it." For one who is so intent on fulfilling God's commandments, Samuel conveniently blots out that mitzvah that limits the assignment of guilt to the perpetrator alone. It is found, not coincidently perhaps, but a few verses prior to our maftir reading.

> Parents shall not be put to death for their children, nor shall children be put to death for their parents; only for their own crimes may persons be put to death.
>
> (Deuteronomy 24:16)

Does this mitzvah only apply to Israelites, and not those seen as outsiders, "others"? Could we say, as they said of Amalek, that Samuel did not "fear God"? Perhaps he is the one who should have abdicated his position of leadership and not King Saul.

In sum, however, what we have here is an exchange of roles. In the wilderness, it is the powerful Amalek attacking the vulnerable Israelites. Once in the land, it is the powerful Israelites who attack the vulnerable Amalekites. Is Israel the new Amalek, powerful and cruel? Has Amalek become the new Israel, weak and helpless?

King Saul massacred innocent Amalekites, not for what they did, but for who their ancestors were; and that animus toward a onetime enemy is to be preserved, as our maftir portion says, even when "Adonai your God has given you rest from all your enemies on every hand, in the land that Adonai your God is giving you as an inheritance to possess." Is this not a recipe for distrust and even fear of the vulnerable "stranger" who lives in our midst? Is it too much to expect that one of Saul's attacking soldiers should have cried out: "Stop! We are fighting the ghost of Amalek, and killing real people, his innocent descendants." Have the Israelites, once commanded to "remember what Amalek did to you on your journey out of Egypt," become bifurcated beings, "grasshoppers" in their heads, and "giants" in their bodies?

Perhaps the commands "remember!" and "do not forget!" are best understood as: "Remember" the experience of vulnerability in the wilderness; and "do not forget" how readily the oppressed one can become the oppressor once in the land.

As if this material were not troubling enough, with Purim we go from King Agag the Amalekite in our haftarah portion, to one of his descendants, Haman the Agagite in our megillah (the scroll of the Book of Esther), that fanciful and psychologically revealing text. Fanciful, because Jews, vulnerable, marginal, and denounced to the king as potential traitors, are, wonder of wonders, not harmed. The notion that a Persian monarch gives Jews free reign to kill thousands of Persians is, surely, the stuff of vengeful fantasy. And this is psychologically revealing, because it suggests that the Jews of Shushan see themselves as both an endangered and vulnerable people and a powerful and bloodthirsty one.

First, the Persian Jews are mortally threatened by the Amalekite Haman yimach sh'mo v'zichro (may his name and memory be erased) who connives "to destroy, to kill, and to annihilate all Jews, young and old, children and women ... and to plunder their goods." (Esther 3:13) Who among us, post-Holocaust Jews, does not feel a horrid chill at this language?

Once the tables are turned, however, and the Jews assume power and influence in the court, it is Mordecai who uses the exact same language in permitting the Jews "to destroy, to kill, and to annihilate any armed force of any people or province that might attack them, their children, and their women, and to plunder their goods." (8:11)

While the Jews are perhaps traumatized though not actually harmed by Haman, they, in turn, "struck down all their enemies with the sword, slaughtering and destroying them, and did as they pleased to those who hated them." (9:5)

In the megillah, the Jews personify both the weak and vulnerable Israelites of our Deuteronomy text, and the powerful forces of Saul killing "man and woman, child and infant ... (destroying) all the people with the edge of the sword" (1 Samuel 15:3, 8) of our haftarah. In this one megillah text, Jews are both weak and powerful, victims and oppressors, grasshoppers and giants, Mordecai and Haman. We see here that a traumatized psyche can, in time, give birth to misguided fantasies of murderous revenge.

Haman and Mordecai are presented as polar opposites, one a nefarious Amalekite deserving of our scorn and our raucous efforts to "blot out" even the mention of his name during our reading of the megillah, and the other a proud and courageous Persian Jew, worthy of Purim costume emulation by untold generations of children. They are, however, unfortunately similar in their opportunistic and arbitrary abuse of power and their lack of concern and empathy for those they wish to harm.

Our Torah and haftarah readings for this Shabbat Zachor, along with the upcoming reading of the megillah, alert us to the very real danger of developing a type of moral schizophrenia in which those once oppressed cannot fully escape a sense of their vulnerability, to the detriment of those over whom they will come to have power. We are, I think, at our best when we remember what it was like to be oppressed in Egypt but not to forget that we are no longer there. To think and behave otherwise would be a clear sign to others and to ourselves that we have not yet been liberated from bondage.

"You shall not wrong or oppress a resident alien, for you were aliens in the land of Egypt" (Exodus 22:21) is Torah's great challenge to us, that we might have empathy for others. Living up to that challenge can be quite another matter.

Our Fragile Ship

The Book of Jonah, read in synagogues on the afternoon of Yom Kippur, the Day of Atonement, seems to focus only on Jonah, the most peculiar and reluctant of biblical prophets. The moral crux of the book, however, is the behavior of the anonymous sailors on the boat Jonah boards to flee from his prophetic mission. For unlike Jonah, they believe in the essential worth of human beings and risk their lives to act on that conviction. It is this behavior, and not that of Jonah, that makes this scriptural reading appropriate for this most holy of days. Read about Jonah getting swallowed by a "big fish" if you wish, but not before you pay close attention to the book's opening chapter.

Haftarah for Yom Kippur afternoon—the Book of Jonah

Now the word of Adonai came to Jonah son of Amittai, saying: "Go at once to Nineveh, that great city, and cry out against it, for their wickedness has come up before me." But Jonah set out to flee to Tarshish from the presence of Adonai. He went down to Joppa and found a ship going to Tarshish; so he paid his fare and went on board, to go with them to Tarshish, away from the presence of Adonai.

(Jonah 1:1-3)

The Book of Jonah is a strange choice for the afternoon service nearing the end of ten days of teshuva (repentance for sins of the past year) and Jonah is a very strange prophet. On one level, the portrait of Ninevites at the end of the book, seeking atonement for their misdeeds through fasting, as Jews do, and covering themselves in sackcloth, as Jews do, in a way, through the wearing of a kitel, a white shroud-like garment, seems to fit the mood and theme of Yom Kippur.

On another level, Jonah barely qualifies as a prophet, especially one suited for Yom Kippur. True, God speaks to him and gives him a mission, but he runs away from it, going east to Tarshish instead of west to Ninevah. Unlike other Hebrew prophets, particularly Isaiah, whose urgent and lengthy poetic cry for social justice is a high point of the earlier atonement service this morning, Jonah's total prophetic message is short and dark: "Forty days more, and Nineveh shall be overthrown." (Jonah 3:4) Isaiah wants the Israelites to atone for their sins and change their behavior. But they do not. Jonah doesn't want the Ninevites to obey God's word, but they do, confounding and gravely disappointing him.

So the Book of Jonah seems to leave us with two disparate models for Yom Kippur: non-Israelites who do teshuvah, and a very minor Hebrew prophet whose behavior and lack of empathy threatens other people's lives.

Indeed, it is hard not to see an inverse relationship between the actions of the Ninevites and those addressed by Isaiah's prophetic words. (Isaiah 57-58) Isaiah condemns the Israelites for seeking God's blessings through fasting and lying down in sackcloth and ashes, yet persisting in their wicked ways, while the Ninevites, though likewise fasting and covering themselves with sackcloth, genuinely atone for their sins by departing from their immoral behavior.

Strange, indeed, this Book of Jonah and our associations with it: teshuvah-doing Ninevites and hypocritical Israelites; a reluctant, non-empathic Jonah and an Isaiah who is so articulately passionate about social justice. It is within the context of these contradictions that I suggest we pay careful attention to the sailors Jonah encounters on the way to Tarshish. Indeed, they are the main actors of the entire first chapter of this brief book and it is through their actions, their words, and their questions that I see the essential message of this haftarah reading.

> But Adonai hurled a great wind upon the sea, and such a mighty storm came upon the sea that the ship threatened to break up. Then the sailors were afraid, and each cried to his god. They threw the cargo that was in the ship into

the sea, to lighten it for them. Jonah, meanwhile, had gone down into the hold of the ship and had lain down and was fast asleep.

(Jonah 1:4-5)

The ship is the sailors' whole world. It is where they live and work. On the high seas, they and their world are vulnerable to forces beyond their control. When their world is endangered, they respond in an "all for one and one for all effort," regardless of their place of origin or their religious beliefs or practices. They may not be responsible for the storm, but they are certainly responsible for the well-being of one another and the safety of their ship.

But Jonah, whether out of fear, guilt, indifference, or a narrow nationalism that doesn't concern itself with the well-being of "others," flees once again from responsibility. For him, what happens to the sailors and the ship is acceptable collateral damage for his self-absorbed behavior. But the world comes calling for him nonetheless. He may want to sleep through the storm, but the collective ethic of the sailors insists that he wake up.

> The sailors said to one another, "Come, let us cast lots, so that we may know on whose account this calamity has come upon us." So they cast lots, and the lot fell on Jonah. Then they said to him, "Tell us why this calamity has come upon us. What is your occupation? Where do you come from? What is your country? And of what people are you?"

(1:7-8)

When Jonah's irresponsible behavior is revealed by lottery, the sailors surprisingly do not rush to judgment and demand punishment, actions one would understand for his putting them and their ship in danger. Rather, they interrogate him, repeatedly. They want to know him as a person and not as an object of scorn. They engage him in dialogue.

> "I am a Hebrew," he replied. "I worship Adonai, the God of heaven, who made the sea and the dry land." Then

> the men were even more afraid and said to him, "What is this that you have done!" For the men knew that he was fleeing from the presence of Adonai, because he had told them so. Then they said to him, "What shall we do to you, that the sea may quiet down for us?" For the sea was growing more and more tempestuous.
>
> (1:9-11)

Jonah admits that he is not one of them, in religion or nationality, and that he is indeed responsible for their peril. Yet even in questioning him, the sailors are careful not to victimize Jonah. Indeed, they grant him decision-making power: You tell us what to do!

> He said to them, "Pick me up and throw me into the sea; then the sea will quiet down for you, for I know it is because of me that this great storm has come upon you." Nevertheless, the men rowed hard to bring the ship back to land, but they could not, for the sea grew more and more stormy against them.
>
> (1:12-13)

Now, surely, we would expect a dramatic resolution to the situation: Jonah admits responsibility for the storm and commands the sailors to save themselves and the ship by throwing him overboard. There seems to be no other choice, and they would surely be justified in following his advice. But once again the sailors confound our expectations, choosing to further risk their own lives rather than causing Jonah to lose his until they finally have no choice, and with hearts heavy and a sense of moral failure, they accede to Jonah's wishes:

> So they picked Jonah up and threw him into the sea, and the sea ceased from its raging. Then the men feared Adonai even more, and they offered a sacrifice to Adonai and made vows.
>
> (1:15-16)

Now, at the very end of this first chapter, the words and actions of these anonymous sailors are summarized in one phrase: The men "feared Adonai." That is a term that Torah and some of its commentators reserve for those whose behavior is shaped not by conformity to external dictates or societal pressure, but by an individual's moral conscience. It is, I think, not mere coincidence that we find this same term in the Torah portion chosen by progressive congregations for Yom Kippur afternoon:

> You shall not revile the deaf or put a stumbling block before the blind; you shall fear your God: I am Adonai.
>
> (Leviticus 19:14)

In a situation where you could ignore the needs or the human dignity of a blind or deaf person and get away with it, you should know in your heart that that is not the right thing to do, and that you should rather "fear your God," that is, be guided by an independent moral compass.

The sailors could have retaliated against Jonah with impunity. They could have ostracized him, demeaned him, and sought immediate and even violent revenge against this inconsiderate source of their dangerous situation. But they did none of this, for these non-Israelites, people Torah might otherwise consider immoral idol worshippers, were yiray Adonai, those who fear God, and each and every one of them knew what the right, good, just, decent, and caring thing to do was, and they did it.

We remember that there were other non-Israelites whose moral behavior led them to help vulnerable Hebrews. The Egyptian midwives Shifra and Puah exemplified this behavior when they defied Pharaoh's orders to kill newborn Hebrew males—and are said to "fear God." (Exodus 1:17) And King Abimelech of Gerar (Genesis 20:11) expressed this fear of God in extending hospitality to both Abraham and Isaac, contrary to their expectations that he would take advantage of their vulnerability as strangers.

These men and women, some named and others anonymous, seemingly incidental figures in the Jewish sacred narrative, are shown to be moral exemplars, models for righteous behavior. More recently, we have come to call those non-Jews who followed a moral conscience in protecting Jewish lives in times of murderous oppression, as some Christians and others did during the Shoah (the Holocaust), chasiday umot ha-olam, righteous ones among the nations.

The anonymous sailors who figure so prominently in the Book of Jonah present us with such a moral model and a challenge. Indeed, it seems that they are the true prophets in our haftarah, and not Jonah. As individuals they acted for the common good; they "feared God" and behaved morally even when they were not compelled to do so. At a time when their fragile world was gravely threatened, they treated a stranger as one of their own for as long as they were able to do so.

Jonah did not deserve a book named after him, and it is only so, I suggest, because his name appears in the book's first few words, as is the case with the weekly parshiyot. A more fitting title might have been the opening words of the fifth verse: "Then the sailors were afraid." They were fearful that their fragile vessel would be destroyed, and rightly so. But also fearful that in combating the storm, they might act in ways contrary to the demands of their moral conscience.

This, I suggest, is a powerful message for us, as we read this portion while our ten days of introspection are drawing to a close each year. All of us, in our community, in our society, and on this planet are likewise in a very fragile vessel, increasingly tossed about and endangered by forces beyond our individual control. Like the sailors, we are properly fearful that our vessel might break apart, and that we, and all whom we love and care for, might suffer grave consequences.

But in combating our storm, may we also be fearful of acting in ways contrary to the demands of our moral conscience. So may we learn from our haftarah that our individual well-being demands a collective and inclusive struggle, that we, in this world of disparate tribes and far-flung nations, might yet keep our fragile ship from foundering, and together bring it home to a safe and peaceful harbor.

Unholy Violence

This sermon was delivered to students and faculty of DePaul University on Erev Yom Kippur in 2000. It was at the beginning of what was called the Second Intifada, a Palestinian uprising against Israeli occupation of the West Bank and Gaza. It was a time of increased violence in an Israel that was close to my heart and where I had friends and acquaintances. This was my cry for peace and justice. With very few changes, I would again share the same words and the same tears, now almost a quarter of a century later.

Erev Yom Kippur 2000

I sit at my desk surrounded by news reports, editorials, and feature stories from the American press and Israeli sources. Events unfold, selectively seen, partially understood: Who is right? Who started it? Who is to blame? Who is a murderer, a liberator, a provocateur? The answers depend upon who you ask, whose account you read: pro-government or anti; religious or not; Palestinian or Israeli; teenager or elder.

I sit at my desk in these days between Rosh Hashanah and Yom Kippur, these days of teshuvah, of turning toward atonement—and I don't know which way to turn. Frozen in one camera's lens and in my mind's eye is the twelve-year-old Palestinian boy Mohammed al Duri, his bullet-riddled body slumped alongside the father who could not protect him. Grasped firmly in another lens is the bloody face of twenty-year-old Tuvia Grossman, beaten and stabbed on his way to pray at the Western Wall. It was on Shabbat, which is supposed to be a day of peace—a taste, our rabbis say, of olam ha-ba, the world to come. It was on Rosh Hashanah, yom harat olam: the birth day of the world, so say the rabbis.

It was the day we opened our Torah to that place where Father Abraham separated his two sons. The one named Ishmael he sent into the wilderness, westward from Be'er Sheva, perhaps to die. The one named Isaac he takes north to Moriah, land of hills and thickets, binds him tightly to a rocky altar and prepares to slaughter him. Ishmael is rescued at the final moment by an angel and becomes a people, aravim, those of the West, Arabs of the land of the Philistines, Palestinians. Isaac is angelically rescued as well, surviving to become those of yahud, of Judea, the Yehudim, the Jews.

Still blood flows.

Angels don't live here anymore. The boy Mohammed al Duri died west of Be'er Sheva, in Gaza, and Tuvia Grossman was beaten on his way to the Wall at Moriah, the mountain where Isaac's altar-rock still sits, the very one on which the mikdash, God's house, the Temple in Jerusalem, was built, so say the rabbis. It now rests under the dome of a mosque on Haram al Sharif—in Al Quds, the holy city, Yerushalayim, Jerusalem.

The rock is huge. Even in a rocky land, it calls attention to itself. Before the time of the Israelites it was holy, to one god or another. Elijah prayed there, and King David, and Solomon, so say rabbis and imams alike—and the prophet Mohammed launched himself into heaven from that spot, a spot on which has stood a Jebusite shrine; the mikdashim, the Jewish Houses of God; a Roman temple to Jupiter; a Christian basilica; a masjid, the present Mosque of Omar. Holiness is contagious; it flows so subtly and yet so surely from one religion to another, each claiming sole rights of possession. Like a magnet, it draws events to it, real and imagined—for rocks in this part of the world are symbols of power and eternity, tsur Yisrael, O Rock of Israel (we call our God); and St. Peter, Petra, is the rock upon which the Church is said to have been founded. Blood stains the rocks of Moriah: that of the lambs of sacrifice, the korbanot of Yom Kippur. Crusaders flooded the narrow streets with Jewish and Muslim blood—cleansing the land of the infidel, so they said.

Still blood flows.

What of Be'er Sheva, city of Abraham, east of Gaza and south of Jerusalem, between Mohammed al-Duri in one direction and Tuvia Grossman in another? What of Be'er Sheva, the "well of the oath," where, says our Torah, Isaac and the Philistine leaders swore a treaty of peace, that they and their peoples will not harm or molest one another, but deal kindly and so be blessed? (Genesis 26:28-29) Shalom, shalom, v'ain shalom, the prophet Jeremiah (6:14) cries out in the wilderness: "Peace, peace, but there is no peace," for blessing is not yet ours.

Tomorrow morning we open our Torah and read of ritualized atonement for sin: take two goats, males and unblemished, choosing by lottery which shall live and which shall die.

> When he has finished atoning for the holy place and the tent of meeting and the altar he shall present the live goat. Then Aaron shall lay both his hands on the head of the live goat and confess over it all the iniquities of the Israelites, and all their transgressions, all their sins, putting them on the head of the goat and sending it away into the wilderness by means of someone designated for the task. The goat shall bear on itself all their iniquities to a barren region, and the goat shall be set free in the wilderness ... The one who sets the goat free for Azazel shall wash his clothes and bathe his body in water and afterward may come into the camp.
>
> (Leviticus 16:20-22,26)

That goat (released to the wilderness and thus referred to as an "escape-goat") is sent to Azazel, traditionally a place of the demonic or hell. A second goat, the holy sacrifice to God, is slaughtered on the altar-rock, its blood sprinkled on the horns of the altar to purify it from the sins of the Israelites. Its carcass, however, is dumped outside the camp. It has, paradoxically, become impure in the purification process, so it must be destroyed by fire.

Blood again. A blood ritual for atonement, but contaminating, polluting, defiling none the less. Atonement by scapegoating, vicariously, by killing the other, the sinful one, the enemy. Is that to be the way of cleansing, and new beginnings? Is bloodshed its necessary price, which, in turn, defiles the shedder of blood? What are we in our time to make of the rabbis' interpretation of these two goats: one a reparation for Ishmael sent into the wilderness burdened with the sins of the people; one an atonement for Isaac, fit for holy sacrifice, his blood to be spilt on the rock Moriah for the purification of his people?

Later, the practice in Jerusalem will be to lead the scapegoat from the house of God, from Moriah, not to the wilderness to be released, but down a rocky path, to be hurled over a steep precipice, its body broken on the sharp rocks below. No danger now that it can return, to haunt the people with their own sins. Such psychiatrists, our rabbis, intuiting long before Freud the fear of "return of the repressed," the ultimate failure of scapegoating as true cleansing.

I sit at my desk and think of the land, sighing in remembrance of my time in ha-Galil, the Galilee, fires now ripping through her carefully planted hillsides, main roads blocked as guns meet rocks, Arab blood flowing, and Jewish blood. The Palestinian-identified Israeli Arabs no longer quiet or cooperative, explode resentment into hateful stone-throwing over years of discrimination and second-class citizenship. Each people will trumpet their wounded, their dead, their shock and grief, their frustration and incomprehension. Who is to blame? Who has pieces of the whole, bits of truth?

I think of ha-Galil sheli, my Galilee, which was never really mine but rhetorically. To whom do you belong, really, and by what right? Of arms, or settlement, or history, or God? And what of those Arab villages that may have Talmudic names, and whose Jewish farms may be on Arabic family land? To whom do you truly belong?

Two peoples in one land, both calling Abraham/Ibrihim their father and both claiming a rightful inheritance. Can brothers really be separated? Even goats know enough to come back when exiled. So do brothers, each to reclaim a rightful possession, a promised land, a homeland, that which can never be forgotten no matter how long the exile or difficult the struggle—that for which one is prepared to kill, and, if necessary, die.

I remember a summer, now thirty-six years ago and before Jerusalem's boundaries changed and the Wall was opened to Jews. At that time, we had to look over the barbed wire and rock-strewn border between "their" Jerusalem and "ours" to even glimpse the Wall. I yearned to walk the streets of that ancient city, descend to the Wall of Jewish tears, caress her stones, and be close to God. Above the Wall, on Moriah itself, was the rock where the holy of holies had been, at the very center of the House of God, where the high priest on Yom Kippur would utter the four-lettered name of the Holy One of Old, and save the people from their sins for another year. That rock, say the rabbis, was where Isaac was bound. I had yet to learn that Muslim tradition that sees Ishmael as the son Abraham bound on the altar of Moriah for sacrifice.

Two sons, two peoples, bound by the father they had in common, on the same rock, at God's command—or so Abraham/Ibrahim thought.

My modern, rational spirit is haunted by the image: Isaac and Ishmael, Israeli and Palestinian, each bound to the rock of Moriah, the holy mount, the Wall of tears. Their peoples, Jews and Muslims, both of whose religious teachings prohibit any material representation of the sacred as idolatrous, and which see the worship of stones and trees as an abomination, have yet to unbind themselves from the rocky altars upon which their parents and ancestors have laid their spirits and their bodies. It is time, it is long past time, for rabbis and imams to liberate their peoples from the deceptions and misrepresentations that have long clouded their religious vision and their moral judgment.

Questions of priestly manipulation and control of holy sites aside, the attributing of ultimate value to holy stones comes at the price of scapegoating and violence. When stones are valued more than human life, when holy spaces are purchased at the expense of dispossessing or oppressing those who are seen as rivals with whom the land cannot be legitimately shared, then the moral and spiritual depth that is possible within each religious tradition is sacrificed, and the goodness and integrity of both peoples is gravely diminished.

In her book, *The Curse of Cain*, Regina Schwartz calls this kind of thinking "agonistic," in which a sense of identity is developed against or antagonistic to another person or religion or nation. It is a way of constructing identity that is, she claims, intrinsic to the Bible, its teachings, and its values.

In this way we may come to define ourselves not only by virtue of who we are, but by who we are not: Hebrews and not Egyptians; Israelites and not Canaanites; the am segulah, the "chosen people," and not the goyim asher lo y'da-ucha, those people who do not know you, the one, true God. It is, however, a dangerous road for a people to travel, leading to exclusive claims to land, to boundaries drawn in blood, and to permissive acts of violence against the "other." It is based on the assumption that there are insufficient resources for sharing; the land, the blessing, the sacred places, the promised future, must all be possessed by one side or the other, one brother or the other, one people or the other.

In Torah, this value is played out in a succession of narratives: God seemingly cannot choose the offerings of both Cain and Abel; Cain's offering is arbitrarily rejected; in a rage he murders his brother, and, in turn is exiled from the land. Abraham and his nephew Lot cannot pasture the same land: one goes west toward Jerusalem, the other east, toward the Jordan. Isaac and Ishmael are ripped apart as children, lest their father's inheritance be shared. Jacob steals his brother's blessing, and Esau harbors murderous thoughts of revenge. Only Israelites are to settle in the Promised Land; the Amorites, Hittites, Jebusites, and the other inhabitants of Canaan are to be cast out, violently; the land cannot be shared.

And so it goes, in the Israel of those days, and these, each people claiming, in the name of unique identity and exclusive inheritance, that, as Schwartz puts it, "its right to the land is historical, and divine." Or, as our rabbis have said: The land belongs to God, who can take it from one people and give it to another, as God sees fit. The intent is clear, and irrevocable—our God takes the land from them and gives it to us, a divine mandate, as Rashi comments on the opening verse of Genesis. For claims of ultimate authority are rarely open to rational discussion, negotiation, mediation, or compromise.

The prophet Isaiah cries out in the wilderness:

> Many peoples shall come and say, "Come, let us go up to the mountain of Adonai, to the house of the God of Jacob, that he may teach us his ways and that we may walk in his paths." For out of Zion shall go forth instruction and the word of Adonai from Jerusalem. He shall judge between the nations and shall arbitrate for many peoples; they shall beat their swords into plowshares and their spears into pruning hooks; nation shall not lift up sword against nation; neither shall they learn war any more.
>
> (Isaiah 2:3-4)

But who listened to prophets in those days—and where are they now when we so urgently need their voices and their vision?

You may call my reflection here naïve. I write from a distance, where my home is not threatened, my child not endangered. Perhaps it is not my place to tell those whose lives are under siege how best to defend themselves and protect their children. And yet, can I remain silent? I feel so deeply that Israel is my homeland, her soil my soil, her people my people. I also feel that Jewish blood is no redder, no purer, no less precious than Palestinian blood. I know that Palestinian parents are no less caring for the life and the future of their children than Jewish parents, nor in any less agony when their children are threatened, or harmed, or killed.

And I wonder: Where are the voices of rabbis and imams in a land where prophets and saints once cried out for peace and justice for all peoples? Where are the courageous proponents of those compassionate and caring values that both Judaism and Islam claim as an inheritance? Where are the visionaries who can imagine a world beyond the bloody and hateful present and work passionately and ceaselessly to make that vision a political and social reality? Where are the spiritually compelling voices of those who ought properly to challenge their own people to consider that rocks and stone walls, however sanctified by time and tears, are, in the end, just rocks and stone, and that it is human beings—and only human beings—that are of ultimate value?

Schwartz has it right, I think. If we create identities agonistically, by stressing the difference between ourselves and those we label as "other," and if we see them primarily as not one of us—as less than and less deserving than we are—then we open wide the path toward treating "them" with indifference, or cruelty, or violence. And if they, likewise, use us as scapegoats, demeaning our identity and our rights, then they can, and will, treat us in similarly dismissive and violent fashion.

When will we finally listen to the prophet who dares to speak to people and politicians across twenty-eight centuries in the name of God?

> I hate, I despise your festivals, and I take no delight in your solemn assemblies. Even though you offer me your burnt offerings and grain offerings, I will not accept them, and the offerings of well-being of your fatted animals I will not look upon. Take away from me the noise of your

songs; I will not listen to the melody of your harps. But let justice roll down like water and righteousness like an ever-flowing stream.

(Amos 5:21-24)

Will You Forgive Me?

Whatever your faith and whatever your perspective may be on Torah, I hope that this journey leaves you eager to engage with scripture full of the questions we all have each day of our lives. That is why I am closing this book with my most personal sermon, one I shared with the Lomdim Minyan at the end of our Ten Days of Atonement, Yom Kippur morning, in 2012. Though my father had been dead for over twenty years, I had yet to lay him to rest in a psychological and spiritual sense. So on that morning, with my dear community as witnesses, I resolved to do so, asking for his forgiveness for sins I may have committed against him. I like to believe that he has forgiven me—and I hope that this final chapter will resonate with you, as well, as you contemplate your own spiritual journey with those who surround your life.

Yom Kippur morning

For transgressions between persons, atonement only comes when we forgive one another.

(Mishnah Yoma 8)

In a very small corner of Cedar Park cemetery in Oradell, New Jersey, lies my family: grandparents, aunts and uncles, a first cousin. My father has been there for over twenty years. Ours had been a difficult relationship. We grew up in different worlds and spoke different languages when we did speak, which was rarely. His death left me with a sense of unfinished business. I have, I think, wronged him, in words and in deeds. As an act of teshuvah (atonement) I feel a need to speak to him, to ask his forgiveness, to bring some sense of closure to our relationship.

In seeking atonement from one who is dead, our tradition suggests taking a minyan (ten Jews) to the gravesite and begging for forgiveness. But that would, it seems, be well beyond even our minyan's logistical capacities. What I could do, however, is bring my father here, and ask for his forgiveness in the presence of this community.

So allow me to introduce my dad. My father's name was William; everyone called him Bill; on the birth certificate he reluctantly showed me late in his life, he is Hayim Wolf.

I knew him to be a strong, self-confident, clever man. He was as skilled in business as he had long been in athletics—and fearlessly competitive in both. But this man, gentle and sweet though he would often be, had a temper, which spontaneously erupted from time to time, much to my disadvantage.

But it is more what my father wasn't that has troubled me for so long, than what he was. I wanted an intellectual for a father, highly educated, culturally sophisticated, and widely traveled. What I got was a man who may not have graduated high school, was culturally uninterested, and intellectually unsophisticated. He rarely read a book, and had no interest in music, or dance, or theater that I was aware of. He was a homebody, parochial. He never traveled much beyond New York City and, with retirement, Delray Beach, Florida.

Beyond this, it was my father, the Jew, who disappointed me. I wanted a father who was a proud, knowledgeable, and practicing Jew, handing down the wisdom of our tradition as Jews have for millennia, generation after generation, father to son. I wanted a father who sat, dressed in his Shabbat finery at the head of our dinner table, leading us in the berachot (blessings), teaching us nigunim (wordless melodies), sharing the depths of Torah with us, putting his hands on my head, blessing me in the name of Ephraim and Menashe. But my father, who had little regard for Shabbat observance, who didn't know berachot or nigunim, who had no Torah to pass down to his children, would work late in his New York City retail store Friday nights—and all day Saturday. Shabbat was not on the radar of his life. With a father like mine, I would have to discover my own melodies, acquire Torah on my own, and strive for blessings elsewhere.

I wanted a father who would be my davvening (praying) mentor in shul (synagogue) against whose tallis (prayer shawl) I would lean, proudly, as he confidently chanted the daily and holiday tefilot (prayers)—but, alas, shul was not a place in which he would likely be found. He knew neither the prayers, nor their Hebrew. He never owned a tallis. With a father like mine, I would have to nurture my own davvening skills and shul confidence.

I wanted a father who would lead our family seder, prolonging the hours of our festive meal, pushing us to deeper and deeper understanding of the Haggadah, the symbols of pesach (Passover) and the meaning of liberation from Egyptian bondage. Alas, our family seders were always held elsewhere, led by someone else's father. With a father like mine, I would need to find my own way out of Egypt.

I wanted a father who was emotionally open, who could convey to me, at the times when it counted most in his life and in mine, what he thought and what he felt. Who could wrap his strong arms around me when I needed comforting, hug and kiss me when I needed to know he loved me, shed tears along with the joys and sorrows of his life and mine. But my father was uncomfortable expressing himself physically or emotionally; he withheld himself from intimacy with my sisters and me. For this we suffered, and I think he did, as well.

When I allow myself to do so, I can understand the very different forces and influences at play in his life from those that affected my own. He was among those who bridged the really hard, impoverished, immigrant generation of his parents and that of middle-class economic security. He grew up literally on the streets of New York City, taking nothing for granted, scrapping for every shred of self-esteem that might be within his grasp. Sports may well have kept him from prison, he said, or worse, and he played like his very life depended upon it, with all the moxie his lean 5'7" frame allowed: semi-professional baseball primarily, then Sunday morning handball.

With perseverance, skill, and year after year of long, hard work, mostly in retail sales, he climbed a shaky economic ladder, eventually carrying his whole family along with him, even through those scary years of the Great Depression, which left their scars on him and, indirectly, on me as well. My father, along with so many of his generation of Jews, assimilated to American secular culture. He wanted to succeed in ways his parents could not, for his children, if not for himself, and he was not going to let Jewish practice or Jewish identity stand in his way in an America still riddled with antisemitism.

Despite such a disappointing father, I did manage to learn Torah, explore it, and teach it, critically and passionately. When she was young, my daughter would lean against my tallis, while I davvened. I am a collector of nigunim, Hasidic stories, and midrashim (traditional Torah commentaries). I place my hands on my child's head at the Shabbat table, that she should be blessed like Sarah, Rebecca, Rachel, and Leah. I hug and kiss her and tell her how proud I am of her and how much I love her. I have striven throughout my adult life to form a Jewish identity and participate in Jewish communities of which I can be proud, and which make sense, spiritually, intellectually, and ethically in modern America.

Despite my father's limited world, I managed to become a rabbi, a social worker, and a college professor. I travel the country and the world exploring the lives of people far different from myself, and learning much from those I might otherwise have considered just foreigners, strangers, even enemies.

Having thought for so long that all this had come to me mysteriously, in spite of who my father was and how he lived his life, I now find myself challenging that perception. It's about time, says this process of reexamination and renewal, that I reconsider the connection between who my father was and the person I have become.

When I finally decided to enter rabbinical school, his concern was whether it was a job that paid a living wage. That's the Depression years speaking; that's a cold-water flat in Brooklyn speaking. That's what comes from year after year after year standing on his feet eight to ten hours a day, selling furniture, lamps, and, finally, pictures and their frames. That's a frugal life that bought only what was needed and paid cash on the line, even for a car. If you didn't have it, you didn't spend it. If you spent it, you spent it wisely. And wisely meant housing for his family, education for his children, and a car that worked.

My father never flew high, or far—but he gave me a ledge to leap from, shoulders to stand on, the space for me to flap my wings and fail, and flap again and again, until I flew—solo, and on my own terms.

Now that I allow myself to do so, I am able to see my father, not for what he lacked, but for what he had. I can not only forgive him for not being the father I wanted, I can be proud and appreciative of his values and his accomplishments. I can ask him to forgive me for not being the son I should have been. For a seemingly confident man, my father was quite shy. He didn't speak much, or well. But if he couldn't say "I love you," then I could and should have, meeting him halfway or more. I now regret words not spoken: words acknowledging the difficulties of his early life, the obstacles he needed to overcome; words of appreciation for the opportunities he allowed me to pursue, even if he didn't fully understand why I would want to do so.

So, Hayim Wolf ben Shachna—you for whom I light yahrzeit (memorial) candles, you for whom I say Kaddish (the mourner's prayer): s'lach li, s'lach li, s'lach li—forgive me, forgive me, forgive me.

Having come this far, I now need to challenge myself further. If this process of reassessing and reincorporating a relationship with my father into my life is possible, how might this serve as a model for the emotional and intellectual work I yet need to do, so that I might repair the broken parts of other significant relationships?

On Yom Kippur, we are called to engage in a process of tikkun nefashot, of inner reflection and personal transformation, that we might begin to take those first, difficult steps toward freeing up relationships that may be stuck in the past, at points of disagreement, misperception, or false pride; that we might begin to value others for who they are, uniquely and wonderfully, and tell them so, even with hugs and tears; that we can we begin to ask forgiveness of one another for words spoken or withheld, for actions that hurt, however unintentionally so. If one can do teshuvah with the deceased, we surely must be able to do teshuvah with the living: with our families, our friends, our professional colleagues, and with those who comprise our religious community.

> For transgressions between persons, atonement only comes when we forgive one another.
>
> (Mishnah Yoma 8)

On this Day of Atonement, we are challenged to transform ourselves into the most caring and compassionate persons we are capable of becoming. In doing so, we just may change those in the world around us, and ourselves, as well, a not insignificant goal for the beginning of this new year.

Shana tovah tikatayvu v'tichataymu: May we write and seal ourselves and all whom we care for into the Book of Life for a good, sweet, and joyful new year.

Afterword

(from a Muslim perspective)

In *Torah Wrestling*, Rabbi Roy Furman demonstrates his wise and vibrant storytelling talents as he explores some of the greatest stories in the human experience.

These are timeless stories that are familiar to Jews, Christians, and Muslims—and even to millions who don't subscribe to the Abrahamic faiths. Most of them have become classics of Western culture because of the relatable nature of their respective messages. But do we really understand these stories we have inherited? Are we able to draw on their wisdom? In these pages, Rabbi Furman offers a refreshing and captivating account of those familiar—and some not so familiar—narratives in a way that offers hope and inspiration.

The Austrian-American sociologist Peter Berger defined plausibility structures as those elements that make and maintain functionality for societies. Foremost among these for Berger is religion. No society wakes up in the morning and decides to be dysfunctional as a communal goal. Religion provides the guardrails and circuit breakers to prevent societies from deviating too deeply from its functional trajectory. Religion does so in two ways: by providing a model of historical continuity and by furnishing scripture, which serves as the wisdom of the ancients that worked and can continue to work, subject, of course, to relevant and required interpretation to contemporary realities.

Afterword (from a Muslim perspective)

The stories of the Torah are that wisdom—a wisdom Muslims believe is part of the divine message that has been given to 124,000 messengers, over time and place, to every community on earth. The stories affirm the universality of humanity, and its shared purpose, both to worship the Creator and to fulfill the divine mission in creating a just, ethical society on Earth. In that sense, there is commonality among the Torah, the Qur'an and the Bible more broadly in establishing the required principles for the attainment of such a society, through the wisdom we glean from these stories. And while these stories delineate morals and roadmaps, they also require acknowledgment of a central focus—those members of society that are most vulnerable, most marginalized, most needy of protection from the broader community, especially those most privileged.

A constant thread through Rabbi Furman's wonderful interpretations of scripture is his centering of the "other." Rabbi Furman restores and rehabilitates the key figures of the Torah, and even highlights those that may commonly be, at best, supporting actors in the dramas at hand.

As a Muslim, I was particularly touched by his empathetic account of Hagar. Revered in Islamic narratives, Hagar is the paragon matriarch. It is her experience and example that Muslims commemorate, emulate, and reenact during their pilgrimage, be it the Umrah, or minor pilgrimage, or the fulfillment of one of the Five Pillars of Islam, the annual Hajj. Sadly, Hagar often receives far less attention in many accounts of these ancient stories as they are told and retold outside the Islamic world—and that is why I so welcome Rabbi Furman's assessment of her extraordinary life that presents her in a new light for readers of this book. He shows how Hagar's faith, patience, temperance, perseverance, and courage—despite being alone in the desert with her young child—serve as inspiration for us all.

Critical in appreciating Rabbi Furman's analysis of Hagar is his affirmation of what she was not. He makes it a point to describe her as a non-Israelite, a woman and also a mother. In today's era of tribalism, even hyper-tribalism, the "other" is either ignored or scorned. We engage in such an exercise at our own peril, because it is so dangerously reductive. Rabbi Furman reminds us that we are composed of a multitude of identities, and we can always find common ground with at least one to see the potential of the "other" as the "self."

While people draw spirituality, inspiration, and guidance from so many of the individuals Rabbi Furman cites, it is important to remember that each and every one of them was regarded, at some point, as the "other," even by their own respective communities. Despite being custodians and purveyors of the divine message, they were often welcomed by disdain and derision. Through the stories of Adam, Eve, Noah, Moses, Abraham, and Hagar, among many, Rabbi Furman reminds us that the complacency of presuming the message will be accepted readily elides the reality faced by these figures.

Moses received the Ten Commandments on Mt. Sinai, among them, the warning against taking the Lord's name in vain. Growing up, I was always taught that this meant one should not invoke the divine in some form of condemnatory profanity. But increasingly, it seems this admonition is to avoid invoking God as a means to pass judgment of whether a calamity is a form of divine punishment or good tidings are indicative of providential privilege.

Rabbi Furman makes the strong and important case that the mystery of divine intent remains with the Creator. His overall message upholds the Islamic tenet, *Wa Allahu A'alam*: "And God Knows Best."

Religion was never intended to be an abstract concept, and scripture was never meant to be a collection of esoteric principles, out of reach or applicability by its intended audience. Rabbi Furman shows us that both religion and scripture are addressing those who may be striving for perfection, knowing full well that such a pursuit is presumed unattainable. More importantly is the lesson, and comfort, that God gauges intention, not successful achievement, per se. That offers us succor in a volatile world when few anchors and pillars appear to exist. But it also throws the challenge back to humanity to walk the path without falling prey to despair or ambivalence toward our fellow humankind.

If that requires grappling with the difficult issues, or wrestling with the Torah and other divine scripture—Rabbi Furman shows us how it can be done.

Saeed Khan is Associate Professor of Near East & Asian Studies and Global Studies at Wayne State University, where he is also Director of the Center for the Study of Citizenship. He is also the Co-Founder of the Institute of Social Policy and Understanding, a research center studying American Muslim life.

About the Author

Rabbi Roy Furman is a native of New York, educated at Queens College, and ordained by Hebrew Union College-Jewish Institute of Religion in 1971. His writing and thinking as a rabbi and as a Jew have been influenced by his work with havurot (Jewish fellowship groups), minyanim (prayer groups), and Jewish congregations in Los Angeles, Portland, OR, Chicago, and Evanston, IL; by his Hillel work at the University of Southern California and DePaul University; by his graduate work in the history of religions, ancient Judaism, and early Christianity; by his twenty years of teaching comparative religion and Jewish Studies courses at DePaul; by his training and practice as a clinical social worker; and by his numerous stays in Israel: traveling, working, studying, and doing archaeological work over the course of his adult life. He now lives in Chicago with his wife, Dr. Frida Kerner Furman, a retired DePaul professor of social ethics and religious studies. His daughter, Daniella, is a neuroscientist living in Berkeley, CA with her wife, Yula, and their absolutely adorable child, Ilani.

Connect with Rabbi Roy Furman

If you'd like more information about Rabbi Roy Furman or about *Torah Wrestling*, please visit TorahWrestling.com.

If you'd like to use *Torah Wrestling* for a small group discussion, a free discussion guide is available for download on the website.

If you enjoyed this book, and think that others would find it helpful, please consider leaving a review on Amazon or on Goodreads.com.

To contact Rabbi Roy, please email him at roysfurman@gmail.com.

More Books by Jewish Authors

Torah Tutor
by Rabbi Lenore Bohm

In *Torah Tutor*, Rabbi Lenore Bohm draws on a lifetime of teaching about the Torah, the first five books of the Hebrew Bible, starting with Genesis. Reviewers of the book praise the timeliness of the themes lifted up in this contemporary self-guided study, which is ideal for individual seekers and group discussions.

Finding God in Unexpected Places
by Rabbi Jack Riemer

Widely sought after as a master storyteller and teacher, Riemer is one of the most frequently quoted rabbis in the U.S. That's because of the winding paths he takes in describing the relevance of timeless Jewish wisdom in our modern world. What do a professional baseball player, Elizabeth Taylor's jewelry box, a hurricane, a garbage dump and a blue blazer hanging in your closet have to do with each other? They're all turning points in Riemer's stories.

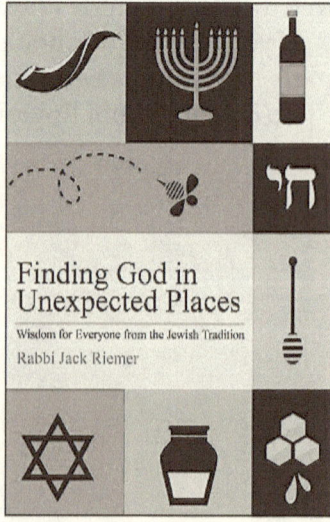

More Books by Jewish Authors

Thanks. I Needed That.
by Rabbi Bob Alper

The Tonight Show, the forests of Vermont, and a tiny Polish village are among the settings for these 32 true stories by Rabbi Bob Alper. This is his latest collection, following an earlier book of stories that a *Detroit Free Press* reviewer called "a volume of spiritual gems." Bob's unique experiences, from leading large congregations to performing stand-up at Toronto's "Muslimfest," make for a wealth of engaging stories.

Life Doesn't Get Any Better Than This
by Rabbi Bob Alper

"Sure. But this might take a while," is how Bob Alper responds when the passenger flying next to him asks what he does. He's a rabbi who earned a doctorate at Princeton Theological Seminary, has performed stand-up comedy hundreds of times with Arab and Muslim comedians, and is heard daily on the Sirius/XM clean comedy channel. This book is a collection of his best true and moving stories.

More Books by Jewish Authors

GodSigns
by Suzy Farbman

Suzy Farbman was a successful author who Oprah introduced to the world as an expert on the tough challenge of saving a marriage. But, behind the scenes, Suzy's world was falling apart after an ominous stager four cancer diagnosis from her doctors. Her warm, suspenseful and often funny journey of mixed disciplines is far from a dead end!

Shining Brightly
by Howard Brown

Silicon Valley pioneer, cancer survivor and interfaith peacemaker Howard Brown shares keys to resilience. He shows us how to reach out through our families, our communities and around the world to form truly supportive connections and friendships. From Howard's career as a Silicon Valley entrepreneur, to his conquering metastatic stage IV cancer twice, to his compassionate outreach as a peacemaker, to his love of sports—this ultimately is not one man's story.

More Books by Jewish Authors

This Jewish Life
by Debra Darvick

In this book, fifty-five voices enable readers to experience a calendar's worth of Judaism's strengths—community, healing, transformation of the human spirit and the influence of the Divine. Within these pages are stories of joyous engagement and poignant loss. Readers will meet a teen who followed the path of Judaism after a chance encounter and men and women who turned to Judaism in their struggles with drug addiction and spousal abuse.

100 Questions and Answers about Jewish Americans
by The Michigan State University School of Journalism

This simple, introductory guide answers 100 of the basic questions non-Jews ask in everyday conversation. It has answers about Judaism and Jewish culture, customs, identity, language, stereotypes, politics, education, work, families and food. This guide is meant as a quick, introduction for non-Jews who need a starting point to learn about their neighbors and co-workers.

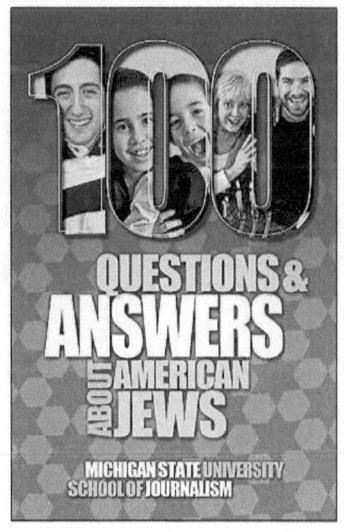

www.ingramcontent.com/pod-product-compliance
Lightning Source LLC
Chambersburg PA
CBHW020933180426
43192CB00036B/898